DEFINABLE MOMENTS

We tend to think of life as a continuum and success as a measurement where we plot progress against time. However, real success is better defined by the wisdom and courage shown for mere moments - moments of meaning that change the trajectory of our lives. These are the moments Andrew explores and helps exploit in 'Definable Moments'. Most importantly, he observes that success requires structure, and then provides a blueprint for readers to build that structure for themselves. Practical. Pertinent. Powerful.

Dan Gregory, CEO
The Impossible Institute

If you've worked with Andrew you'll know the easy part was picking up this book. If you have an aspiration, an achievement that matters to you, you have to do the work that matters. And that's hard. It's so easy to slip back into what's comfortable - but where is the value in that? This book will push you out of your comfort zone as you discover more about the definable moments that are so important for delivering results.

Nola Wakeford, Head of Human Resources
BAE Systems

Andrew has identified that high performance requires making difficult decisions and committing to difficult actions by taking risks, doing the hard yards and paying attention to what really matters. The payoff is worth it. This book will help you to recognise and act on those defining moments to make a difference in your own life and truly realise your potential.

Dr. Susan Inglis, Professor of Practice - Management
LaTrobe Business School

With significant care, wisdom, and fiercely practical knowledge, Andrew mentored me to create a successful career beyond the boundaries of professional cricket. He inspired, empowered and encouraged the specific actions to help make my passion, my future. I am eternally grateful.

Bryce McGain, Director McGain Group
Former Victorian and Australian Cricketer

There is no shortage of inspiration (1%) in the world. Edison made the distinction that perspiration (99%) matters more in success. Andrew has put form to what that work looks like. 'Definable Moments' shows that success is about a series of decisions and a commitment to do the work that matters.

Matt Church, Founder
Thought Leaders Global

Andrew is an exceptional thinker with passion and purpose for life. His excitement and enthusiasm for possibilities are infectious. This inspiring book will help you navigate important choices and is a must read for everyone with a vested interest in their own wellbeing.

Magdalene St. Clare, General Manager
Queensland Association of School Principals

Andrew has a passion and unique capacity to inspire people to be a catalyst for change. He has an incredible ability to fracture fixed thinking and find the issues that require focus. He should come with a danger sign around his neck.

Jackie Allen, HR Director
Bostik

Andrew's common sense coaching and support has been pivotal to the development and success of my business. His practical approach, thought leadership, and easy presence, sets him apart from his peers. Every professional should have someone like Andrew in their corner.

Wendy Fauvel, Director
First Team First

If you want someone who can challenge conventional thinking, and help individuals accept the stretch to work outside their comfort zone to achieve something better, I would highly recommend Andrew.

Carlo Pizzini, General Manager
Pizzini Wines

Andrew's ideas deserve your full attention. This book provides the essential ingredients for success, with content that is practical, thought provoking and performance orientated. It's a must read if you have an appetite to advance.

Gea Zamin, State Manager
MotorOne

'Definable Moment's will give you a life hack around leadership, motivation and your unique way of being. Honest, intelligent and thought provoking, this book delivers on promises resulting in improved performance.

Michael Donahoo, General Manager
Grill'd Healthy Burgers

Published by Brolga Publishing Pty Ltd
ABN 46 063 962 443
PO Box 12544
A'Beckett St
Melbourne, VIC, 8006
Australia

email: markzocchi@brolgapublishing.com.au

All rights reserved. No part of this publication may be reproduced, stored in a retrieval system or transmitted in any form or by any means electronic, mechanical, photocopying, recording or otherwise without prior permission from the publisher.

Copyright © 2017 Andrew Horsfield

National Library of Australia
Cataloguing-in-Publication data
    Andrew Horsfield, author.
    ISBN 9781925367959 (paperback)

 A catalogue record for this book is available from the National Library of Australia

Printed in Australia
Cover design by Workingtype Studio
Typesetting by Elly Cridland

BE PUBLISHED

Publish through a successful publisher. National Distribution, Dennis Jones & Associates
International Distribution to the United Kingdom, North America.
Sales Representation to South East Asia
Email: markzocchi@brolgapublishing.com.au

"This book is an honest, intelligent and thought provoking guide for any leader looking to advance people and performance. It doesn't disappoint."
Michael Donahoo, General Manager, Grill'd Healthy Burgers

DEFINABLE MOMENTS

MASTER THE MOMENTS THAT MATTER IN LIFE AND BUSINESS

ANDREW HORSFIELD

Dedications

To Sarah, Ben and Isabelle. You get the job done every single day and make life fun, full of love and completely fulfilling. This book would not have been written without you. Three magical muses.

Rod and Beth, all that is positive in my life commenced from the platform of your love. You will always have my admiration. Your wisdom, counsel and constant care make me a better man.

Gratitude

Wanting to avoid being in breach of the behaviours I have written about in this book, I have saved writing this section as the final act for finishing the book. My reward for reaching the end, and the chance to recognise the people who have played a role in getting *Definable Moments* published.

This book has taken ten years to write. The last year on the keyboard and the previous nine serving some consistent clients who provided me with the opportunity to develop road test and refine the ideas in this book. Specifically, Rohan Davidson, Mark Sutton, Jackie Allen, Simone Carroll, Nola Wakeford, Simon Clay, Bev Excel, Peter White and Carlo Pizzini. I am grateful to you all and look forward to us continuing to work together as these ideas evolve.

I am indebted to Mark Zocchi at Brolga Publishing for taking a risk ten years ago to publish my first book and supporting this second effort so enthusiastically. Having your knowledge and experience at the helm to put this publication into the market place has been invaluable.

Handing over your hard work to someone to critique can be daunting. Elly, Mark and Julie, your professional editing and input made this process a lot more bearable. The book is the real beneficiary of your work, but a big thank-you from me, and everyone who enjoys reading *Definable Moments*.

My life would be undoubtedly worse off without significant mentors who have generously given their time, counsel, and constructive criticism that helped to shape my perspective. Peter Meaney, you started everything. Thanks Ted Hummerston for two tough questions that kick started some significant conversations.

Mandy Berry you are a superstar. Our life long friendship is the one I treasure most. Matt Church, I forged my own path and value the support you provided along the way. John Devine, my life would be far less meaningful without your care and conversation.

Susan Evans you deserve a paragraph of your own. You have known me the longest and taught me the most. Your constant support, our strong connectedness and brilliant big sister counsel to help navigate decisions, difficulties or direction, has had an immeasurable influence on my life. Probably, more than you know. You are a wonderful woman.

Writing a book is hard work at the best of times, but with two children under two, and the daily demands that are placed on parents, this book would never have been possible without you Sarah. Thanks for accepting time being stretched, and support for Ben and Isabelle sometimes being delayed. You read every word, edited chapters with care, and nurtured the ideas when they escaped me in moments of doubt, fear or tiredness. Marrying you was one of the smartest moves I have made in my life.

Lastly, I want to thank you for supporting this book and being the kind of person who cares enough to read these acknowledgements.

About the Author

Andrew Horsfield is a performance consultant who advises leaders in business, sports and social enterprise. He works exclusively with forward thinking leaders who have work to get done.

Work that shifts the balance, moves things forward, makes a difference and makes results happen.

This work has included turning around disengaged teams and helping people champion organisational change. He has helped professional athletes find another level and worked with leaders under pressure to find clarity amidst complexity. People of influence have also been known to seek out his counsel and considered insight.

With deep expertise in people and performance, Andrew avoids the fist pumping rah-rah that sounds good, but rarely does much good, preferring instead to deliver cutting edge capability development that delivers real world results.

You can find out more at:
www.andrewhorsfield.com

The Definable Moment

/done or finished:-/performance:

A specific point in time in any results-based activity when our aspirations for achievement get seriously challenged. A time people can often feel stuck and performance can stagnate. And the precise moment when high performers put their skills to work to drive the results they deeply desire.

Contents

Dedication

Gratitude

About the Author

The Definable Moment

Introduction		...	1
1.	Better, Not Smarter	...	1
2.	Work Worth Doing	...	23
3.	Success Has Structure	...	49
4.	No Middle Ground	...	75
5.	Build Successful Habits	...	101
6.	Make Motivation Matter	...	125
7.	Do The Work	...	145
Go. Make An Impact.		...	147
Book Philanthropy		...	149

Introduction

Leading
Saying no
Escaping a rut
Making partner
Pitching a project
Finding a fitter you
Running a business
Balancing a busy life
Building a reputation
Making the Test team
Winning the premiership
Smashing the sales record
Creating an inclusive culture
Educating the next generation

The jobs we want to get done are found at the intersection of what matters to us and what needs to change. These are the intersecting moments that we can impact every day, when we choose to pay attention to the things that move us, and motivate us.

This is the work we care about. This is the work worth doing.

Wherever performance exists, successful people, teams and organisations want to make it better. That is what makes them successful. They have a willingness to stretch themselves for something worthwhile. So when it comes to working with people and performance – the one question every client asks me is:

**How do we harness the potential of our people
to drive performance improvement?**

Definable Moments

It's a great question because it demonstrates the aspiration to build a better future and it is probably the reason you picked up this book. You either have a problem you want to turn into performance, or believe that staying stationary is a dangerous posture for success and have an appetite to advance.

Either way, there is a performance gap. There is a discrepancy between where you are, and where you want to be, and this creates tension: positive tension that reflects our aspiration, ambition and desire; and preventative tension that uses fear, distraction and doubt to derail our effort. The presence of tension provides the catalyst for action. But it can also be the point where we become unstuck.

Pursuing what we care about can be daunting because work that is worth doing always has a hard part, a specific point in time when our aspirations for achievement are seriously challenged. This is the time when work can feel difficult, we feel stuck and performance can stagnate. It's also the precise moment we can put our skills to work to deliver the results we deeply desire.

These are the Definable Moments. When these moments come, either we define the moment or it defines us. Success has no middle ground. Choose well and we move forward, choose poorly and we drop back. Don't choose at all and we passively accept whatever comes our way. Putting our skills to work in the moments that matter is a simple idea but not a small idea.

This can fundamentally change the way we work, lead and live.

Accepting responsibility is a challenge because the results we seek usually involves working at the edge of our comfort zone, the place where results take risk, and risk reinforces our preference for safety. But it is clear from every success we see: in the Boardroom, on the sporting field, with the latest start up or the rock star who launches their latest album, those who secure their success learn how to step forward despite the presence of difficulty, doubt or fear.

Once this habit is ingrained we find our freedom.

INTRODUCTION

When we find our freedom, we start making choices, and initiating actions, that serve our results. Making choices changes everything. We become the curator of our own success. The more choices we make, the more momentum we build, and the more opportunities we generate. We realise our gifts, redefine our work and raise the bar. The future is a function of where we put our attention. Employing a structure that promotes a performance orientation is essential to advancement.

SUCCESS HAS STRUCTURE

Failing to structure how we do our most valuable work means we burn energy on low value activities and don't have the energy for the moments that matter, the defining moments when we must overcome the pull of preventative tension and keep making progress. If our energy is not adequately managed, willpower turns into won't power and we stop doing the work that gets the job done.

Performance is impossible when we are unaware of the underlying structures that impact our success. Alternatively, understanding these structures improves our probability for performance. There are three elements that need be aligned for performance to be achieved: Performance, Potential and Interference.

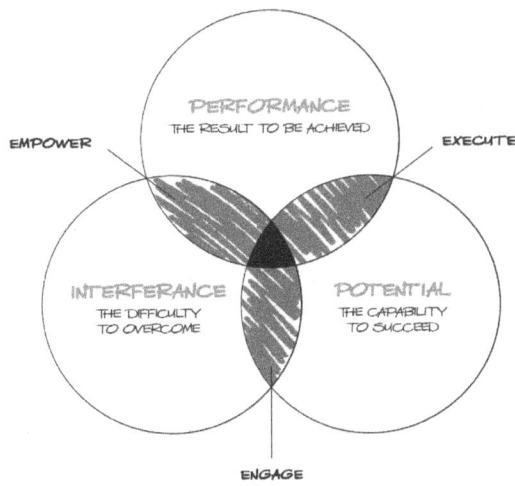

Figure 1: The three essential elements required for peak performance

PERFORMANCE - The result to be achieved
Success starts when we want the promise of the future to be more compelling than the premise of today. Motivation spikes when we are doing meaningful work. When we work to advance a shared purpose rather than protect an individual position or preference. Making our aspiration for achievement captivating can also mitigate the inertia that can occur in moments of difficulty or doubt.

POTENTIAL - The capability to succeed
Potential plummets when we try and mandate certain behaviours to try and make results happen. We excel when work is inherently motivating. Rather than focus on the difficulties or deficiencies that prevent performance being realised, we direct our talents to the work that matters and makes results happen. We invest the assets we have in higher achievement.

INTERFERENCE - The difficulty to overcome
Obstacles play a useful role in any performance-based activity. Without the hard work there would be no value. Identifying the circumstances that can drain our energy and derail our effort, means issues are moved from the subconscious to the conscious, which can then be conquered. We become the creators of our own reality and find the platform to perform our most valuable work.

Maintaining alignment between each of these three components is what makes success so hard to achieve. We might achieve alignment on all of them some of the time, some of them all of the time, but rarely with all of them all of the time. When we experience misalignment, we make the mistake of working on issues in isolation, when in reality they need synchronisation. This imbalance then goes on to create a series of unintended consequences that restrict results being realised:

1. If the Performance to be achieved lacks clarity, or is not compelling, we lack the motivation to make a meaningful contribution, so fail to engage.

INTRODUCTION

2. If we lack the high performance habits that amplify our Potential, we fail to empower the appropriate behaviours required for achievement.

3. If we ignore the Interference that distracts our energy and details our effort, our willpower turns into won't power, and so we fail to execute.

Our ability to identify the definable moments, and be brave enough to impact them, is the key to advancement. Committing our skills to pursue advancement is what enables us to achieve. This rarely presents as a positive opportunity to perform. Most of the time results get disguised in difficult work. Work we choose to seek out if success is a serious aspiration.

FINDING YOUR WAY

We are living in a world where there is an abundance of information, and a shortage of attention. Choose any subject and you can Google it, read about it, download an iPhone application for it or find the seven steps to achieving it. Access to information is abundant and so knowing what to do is no longer the currency of performance. Despite this, we seek out sound-bite solutions and secrets to success because we are time poor and task fatigued.

This book will not provide you with quick fixes or fast solutions.

Great chefs rarely follow recipes. They take the time to understand ingredients. They cook amazing meals by understanding how food works. How it interacts with heat or cold, other flavours, stimulates the palate or is enhanced with seasoning. This book works in a similar way. The pages explore the essential ingredients for advancing performance. Creating the recipe is up to you. Success is too sophisticated to prescribe a simple formula for everyone to follow.

While I suggest you start at the start, finding your own way might mean flicking between chapters that interest you. If that approach works for you, here is an overview of each chapter to help you peruse the parts that matter most to you.

CHAPTER 1 BETTER, NOT SMARTER

The results we seek often take risk. This chapter explores how trying to mitigate risk can lead to seeking out strategies that make us smarter, but not necessarily any better. This results in a performance liability that limits potential.

CHAPTER 2 WORK WORTH DOING

Work worth doing always has a hard part. Difficult moments that can derail the most determined personality, because they stretch our skills, as well as our sanity. Defining these definable moments is the key to advancement and success because it provides the ultimate competitive advantage.

CHAPTER 3 SUCCESS HAS STRUCTURE

When there is a discrepancy between where we are and where we want to be, tension is created. Delivering high performance means maximising performance tension and minimising the tension preventing progress. Understanding how this can be achieved, significantly impacts the results we can achieve.

CHAPTER 4 NO MIDDLE GROUND

Success has no middle ground. Results get realised when we commit ourselves to the moments that matter. This becomes much harder when we relocate our responsibility for results to someone or something else. Delivering results is all about the decisions we make, the actions we take and the outcomes we serve.

CHAPTER 5 BUILD SUCCESSFUL HABITS

Being good some of the time is easy. Being good all of the time is how success gets sustained. This means moving beyond the usual motivational hot air that sounds good but rarely does much good to build a series of habits that help secure new levels of success.

INTRODUCTION

CHAPTER 6   MAKE MOTIVATION MATTER

Feeling a sense of progress fuels performance. When we see the effort we are making is moving things forward, we continue to invest our effort in that work. This chapter highlights the importance of recognising the smaller efforts that make results happen to drive motivation and sustain meaningful momentum.

CHAPTER 7   DO THE WORK

Most of the time results are disguised in difficult work. Work that demands we pursue what matters, stretch our existing skills and forge ahead in the face of doubt. The definable moments which provide a positive opportunity to advance performance.

Being a discerning reader means accepting the invitation to be brave, and recognising the circumstances you need to impact, to achieve what matters to you. The starting point for any meaningful change is being able to see the reality you are creating. Then, accepting the stretch associated with achievement, knowing the results you seek will involve some risk.

Reading, of course, is relatively easy. Acting on ideas is another thing all together. So grab a pen, make notes in the margin, highlight sections, record what inspires you in your journal, or take the idea that arises to a team meeting. Insights are always improved when we take action.

Okay. Here we go.

1
better,
not smarter

Mark Hawwa is helping cure cancer. He is not a Doctor or Research Fellow at a leading university. Nor is he a wealthy businessman acting as a beneficiary to get his name on a building somewhere. He is an Australian entrepreneur who started the Distinguished Gentleman's Ride. A global event that combines dressing dapper, with riding old school motorcycles for a meaningful cause.

The inaugural event in 2012 was a chance for motorbike riders to get together and breakdown some of the stereotypes around men and motorcycles. Attracting over 2,500 riders across 64 cities, the scale and success of the first event made Mark think about how the ride could contribute to a worthy cause. Some key relationships were formed with a focus on prostate cancer and mental health.

Each year the ride has grown in popularity and rider participation. In 2016, the Distinguished Gentlemen's Ride had over 57,000 participants, across 510 cities in 90 different countries. Participants across the various events raised a combined total of US$3.9M for men's health and prostate cancer research.

Mark made his success by having the courage to pursue his passion and turn a possibility into a reality. If you are reading this book, you probably have a similar aspiration. There is something in your life you want to get done.

DO YOU HAVE WHAT IT TAKES?

Of course you do. You have the skills to start. And if you are prepared to take action, and fail forward along the path to success, you will finish. The end may look a little different to what you imagined, perhaps even better, but if you make a start, and commit to the steps that move you forward, you will succeed.

However, if you waste the opportunity, you will fail. Wasted opportunities occur when you wait for more time before you start, wait to find the right way, rather than trust your own way or expect immediate results, before taking a step. Far too often we walk past the opportunities to make an impact. Not because we don't know what to do, but because we don't always have the courage, commitment or willingness to do the work.

Pursuing what we care about can be daunting. When we read a story like Mark Hawwa, listen to a compelling keynote speaker or see a colleague succeed, it's easy to make comparisons and manufacture the myth of not being enough. Not being ready enough, not being smart enough, not being respected enough, not being worthy enough or not being popular enough.

The myth of not being enough arises because we see the best in everyone else and the worst in ourselves. We think the people we see speaking up, taking a risk, living a good life or staying calm in a crisis have something we don't. We deal with this doubt by investing in our authority. Starting more study or seeking out more experience to ensure we are ready to take the step.

The reality is you are ready now. The trick is realising it.

In 1989 Larry (who has since become Lana) and Andy (who has since become Lilly) Wachowski moved to California to make a movie. Now that's not unusual. The cafes and restaurants in California are full of movie hopefuls, waiting on tables, because they chose to make the move and pursue their dream of writing a box office smash.

Movie houses receive over one thousand scripts every week. Of those one thousand scripts, ten get read and reviewed. Of those ten, one is selected for an interview and pitch. At the interview stage, there is only a 6% chance the chosen script will be deemed a worthy investment and made into a movie. Lilly and Lana knew what they were up against and that their dream would be hard work.

They knew Hollywood was full of fantasy science fiction writers who could come up with a script. There are lots of unmade movies in California with potential to make money. What makes the difference to many of those other manuscripts, and Lilly and Lana Wachowski, is that the Wachowski's made *The Matrix*.

When they encountered difficulty, rather than be derailed by it, they used it to drive learning and leverage their success. When their script was criticised they improved it, when they were met with rejection, they called and pitched to a different movie house. When less credible writers got work, rather than complain, they called to ask questions and learn lessons from their success.

Having the commitment and courage to pursue their dream, in the face of set back and struggle, was the difference between Lilly and Lana desiring a box office smash, and delivering a $1.6Bn movie.

Our willingness to do the difficult work, according to Stanford psychologist Carol Dweck, comes down to mindset. The level of belief we have in our ability, and more importantly, whether we believe those abilities can improve.

In her book Mindset: *The New Psychology of Success*, she makes a compelling case that our perception of our ability correlates to our level of achievement. The argument made by Dweck is people can be divided into two categories. Those with a fixed mindset who believe their abilities are hard wired and established, and those with a growth mindset who believe their abilities can be enhanced or improved with effort.

People with a fixed mindset believe their skills are static. You speak well in public, can conquer a Sudoku, but are terrible at reverse parking into a tight space. With a fixed mindset, we believe our skills may vary a little over time, but essentially reflect the way we are wired. People with a fixed mindset tend to avoid really challenging work because they believe being good at something means it shouldn't require too much hard work. The fixed approach connects exertion of effort with a lack of ability, reinforcing a perception of limitation.

Definable Moments

Alternatively, someone with a growth mindset believes abilities can be built and improved with practice. Rather than be dismissive of innate ability, the growth mindset recognises people have different skills and attributes for achievement, however these can adapt and grow with application and experience. Work that challenges current skills, or offers opportunities for learning and growth, tends to be embraced, because it ultimately serves to make us better. Think Roger Federer, after winning eight Open titles, deciding to change his game.

Dweck has applied her mindset theory to Olympic athletes, virtuoso musicians, child educators and business leaders, and her research has clearly shown a difference between fixed and growth mindsets. People with a fixed mindset miss opportunities for improvement and underperform, while those with a growth mindset work to master their abilities, and so continually advance.

In one study, Dweck and two of her colleagues ran an experiment with 373 students who were starting high school. The control group was taught generic study skills, while the experimental group was taught strategies to encourage a growth mindset. Strategies such as: remembering skills they had already learned but at one time were not so accomplished in, and how practice had been a key ingredient to improving those skills. Students were also reminded that 'everything is hard before it is easy' and they shouldn't give up at the first sign of difficulty.

Students in the growth mindset group received a total of two hours training over eight weeks, and the researchers tracked the academic achievements of both the control and experimental group over the next two years. Results for students who received the traditional tuition and study habit training remained the same, while the students receiving growth mindset training experienced a significant uplift to their average grade.

When it comes to doing the difficult work that drives new levels of results, a growth mindset really matters. Our mindset has an increasingly significant effect on the level of success we can achieve. Deciding we have the ability to improve will dictate our efforts and actions. Believing abilities are improvable, means we seek out challenge, stretch our existing skills, and embrace the risk that real results take. We have a preparedness to do the work that enables progress.

Ask anyone you admire who has been able to achieve a level of success and they will tell you self-doubt, set-backs and criticism were a necessary part of pursuing success. It is not the absence of difficulty, but having the skills to manage it effectively, and keep making progress, that makes results happen.

Trying to mitigate the inevitable feelings of fear, doubt and possible failure you will experience along the way, with more learning, will keep you stuck. Learning is the option people pursue to feel like they are progressing without having to take any risk. The real lesson that gets learned is a 'habit of followship' rather than leadership. We become over reliant on investing in other people's ideas.

We rarely need more ideas. We usually need more action.

RESULTS TAKE RISK

All significant accomplishments require risk. When you are starting out and have nothing to lose, or have some sort of safety net, risk is relatively easy to take.

It becomes much harder when the risks pay off and you start to experience success. Having worked hard to experience periods of success and prosperity, you can become complacent. The risks you took to achieve your reward now become the rewards you lose if you take more risk. So you subconsciously protect the status quo and stop doing the very things that made you successful.

This is not a criticism. It is a hard-wired cognitive bias that Neuroscientist Evan Gordon calls the 'fundamental organizing principle of the brain'. As you move through your day, every five seconds your subconscious brain is processing information and asking the one question of evolutionary survival:

Am I safe here?

Definable Moments

Over one million years ago when feeding your family meant encountering danger on a daily basis, this cognitive bias kept us alive. Regularly scanning the environment meant possible danger could be sensed and that helped us stay alive.

When encountering a threat, the fight or flight reaction would trigger certain hormones like adrenalin and cortisol, speeding the heart rate, shunting blood flow to major muscles, changing various other autonomic nervous functions and giving the body a burst of energy and strength to survive.

Despite thousands of years of evolution, where we head to the supermarket rather than having to hunt for our dinner, we still prefer to serve safety and survival. The cognitive bias to assume situations are dangerous, rather than safe, remains. So rather than serve the results we seek, we subconsciously default to the decisions that protect our survival, safety and status.

On the surface, this subconscious hard wiring is often hard to see, and even harder to accept that it's occurring. Exploring the six common characteristics that create our risk aversion is not a solution, but a reasonable first step to see why we stop, when we really need to step:

1. **ANXIETY**

    Anxiety is experiencing failure in advance. Seeing worst-case scenarios and life changing trauma before we have taken a step. If we tell ourselves enough of these stories, they become our reality. A reality that gets limited by fear, doubt and worry. Fear misdirects our attention and prevents us from being our best.

2. **APPROVAL**

    Fitting in with the crowd is safe. So rather than stand out and take the lead we look around for approval: from our boss, our friendship group, the social norms or current state of play. Sourcing a permit before you start your renovations is a good idea. However, the need to seek permission before taking action merely reflects our need for safety. The status quo thinking that keeps us stuck.

3. **AUTONOMY**

   We want to do meaningful work. To enjoy the responsibility of making the decisions that make results happen. But there's the catch. Autonomy isn't given to us. It is something we take. This becomes much harder if we need someone to anoint us before deciding to do something. If the work you want to do, and feel you can do, is proving elusive, perhaps you need to reclaim your autonomy.

4. **ACCOUNTABILITY**

   This is the biggest preventer to advancing performance – not during the good times of course. Everyone is eager to be associated with positive results. But when the challenge arises, obstacles need to be overcome or problems need to be patched up. This is when, all too often, we avoid accountability and relocate the issue to someone or something else. Seeing a set of problems rather than possibilities builds your capability for complaining, rather than controlling.

5. **ACHIEVEMENT**

   Having aspirations for achievement is admirable. However, problems quickly arise when we want the outcome without the work. Success always has a price. If we are not prepared to pay it, we get caught. This is the landscape of late night TV deals telling us we can kick the unwanted kilos by buying the secret formula for just three easy payments of $39.95. Seeking success without the work lures us into fantasy results and false starts that see us lose our way.

6. **ACCOLADES**

   A pat on the back is nice. Recognising progress is a key ingredient to getting things done. However, when we invest our effort with an expectation of return, we stop making commitments and start doing deals. For example, letting someone into traffic but wanting the 'thank you' wave, helping someone move house but expecting a small gift of thanks. Deals are restrictive because people rarely live up to the imaginary bargain we made with ourselves before we began the work.

Taking risks is hard. It has become much harder since popular media started promoting stories selling quick success. The man who had nothing but now drives a Ferrari. The working mum who quit her job and now has a billion dollar business. The singer who bungled his initial audition but ends up winning the talent competition. The overnight success catapulted into fame and fortune. These idealistic stories have distorted our sense of what success really takes.

When we experience struggle, set back or the occasional false start, we get scared. We doubt ourselves. We over-think, over-analyse and over-protect ourselves from the realities of result achievement. It takes hard work. Work we often find hard to do because it occurs at the very edge of our comfort zone.

When you come to terms with the fact that feelings of discomfort and doubt are part of performance, and find your own methods to manage them, you will move forward. Alternatively, when you seek simple solutions or motivational hot air that sounds good, but rarely does much good, you will stay stuck. You may become smarter, but not necessarily any better.

KNOW HOW IS DEAD

If you don't have the right capability you should start there. Everyone needs the right skills to succeed. A pilot needs to know how to land the plane. An engineer needs to know structural dynamics to build the bridge. A personal trainer needs to understand biomechanics to train someone safely. A teacher needs to know explicit instruction for effective classroom management.

The right skills provide the fundamental platform for performance. Most of the time the skills you need have already been sanctioned: you were successful in your interview, you got the second date, you were selected in the team, you were appointed to the Board or your business loan was approved.

Doing the work that drives exceptional results starts by recognising that results get delivered through action. We are now in an economy of connection, attention and collaboration. Choose virtually any subject and you can Google it, read about it, download an App for it or find the seven steps for achieving it.

Access to information is abundant and so knowing what to do is no longer the currency of performance. And this has been true for centuries. Aesop, the ancient fabulist and storyteller, commented on the wealth of information but state of inaction in Greece, in early 564BC, when addressing the Senate.

> *"When all is said and done, more is said, than done."*
> **Aesop**

Acting on the things that matter to you is what creates your results. When you fail to invest yourself in the moments that matter, you develop a performance liability. A gap that gets created when there is a discrepancy between what you know, your *intellectual* capital, and what you do, your *performance* capital.

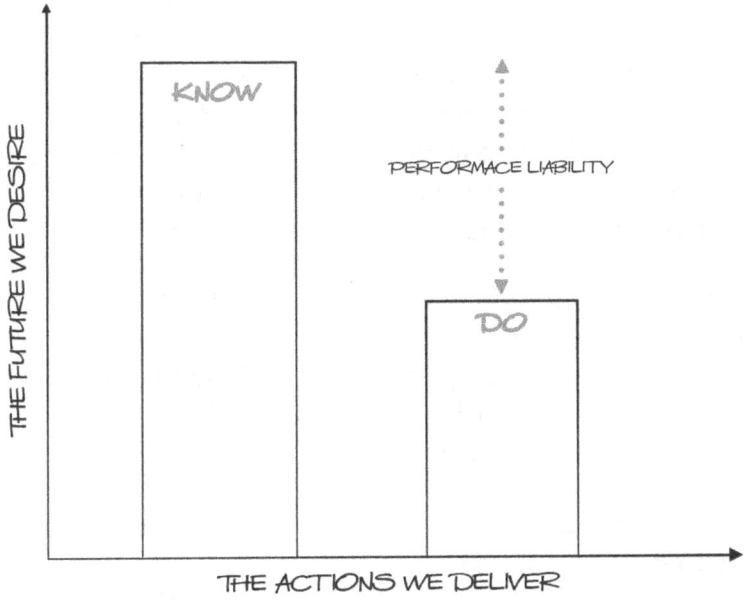

Figure 2: A gap between desiring and delivering creates a liability.

Definable Moments

Our performance liability predominantly presents itself in those recurring moments that make us feel frustrated. These are the times when things are hard, you generally feel stuck and choose to stop. You make the decision, consciously or otherwise, to protect your position rather than pursue high performance.

Here are five real-life examples drawing from ten years of experience as a performance consultant to individuals and industry:

1. An emerging leader disagrees with his leader's direction but doesn't say anything in the meeting. He justifies his decision by telling himself: "Speaking up would be committing career suicide". Instead, he meets a like-minded colleague at a café to complain, missing the opportunity for genuine influence and impact.

2. The Sales team is delivering some good results despite some of the team finding it hard in a difficult market. The real issues of the struggling staff are getting lost in friendly sales banter rather than frank conversations. As a consequence, sales results fluctuate each month as potential clients walk out the door.

3. A woman who was married when she was young is struggling to find the spark in her relationship. She fears a conversation about change might create conflict. So rather than finding the courage to address the issue reasonably, she accepts the status quo missing the opportunity to reignite her life-long relationship.

4. A brilliant young footballer with all the attributes for a successful career is drafted to his favourite club. He is liked immediately by some of the senior players and feels success by association. He doesn't work hard enough, gets delisted and carries the disappointment he feels for his entire life.

5. An engineer with a reputation for delivering results gets promoted to a leadership role. Despite her leadership training, she finds it hard to let go of the day-to-day detail, micromanaging staff and impacting moral. The team feels disempowered so disengage from doing the work they were once delivering.

Our liability develops when we fail to do the meaningful work. Most of the time we try to address our liability by outsourcing the solutions to someone else. We attend a training program, buy more books, listen to the podcast or seek out a trusted advisor for their wise counsel. On face value, each of these options is a reasonable action to take to help move you forward.

But here's the thing. Despite learning more, finding the steps to take, or getting some encouragement, we still remain stuck. This is not because the options we take are unhelpful, it's because the interference we experience is stronger.

- Why do organisations put people through training, investing hours of effort, and thousands of dollars in expense, only to accept when people return, within a matter of days, they default back to their previous behaviours?
- How come leaders who get promoted, and have access to internal programs, systems and support, start by wanting to make a real difference, but end up overwhelmed managing the day-to-day drift rather than delivering results?
- Why do some people with work to do, wait until the last minute, and then rush around in a stressful state, exerting a Herculean effort to get things done, when a controlled approach is more conducive to productivity?

You get the point. When we see a liability as an opportunity to advance, we get ahead. When we deny a liability, missing the moments that move us forward, we stay stuck. Glenn Hansard, without addressing his liability, would just be an Irish busker. Barak Obama, without addressing his liability, would just be a candidate. And Einstein, without addressing his liability, would just be an eccentric inventor.

Situations where we have to make a difficult decision regarding our future occur every day. We decide what we want to commit to. Our willingness to take courage, and commit to the moments that do matter, is the only effective antidote to reducing our liability and realising the results we desire.

REDUCE YOUR LIABILITY

Reducing our liability by putting our skills to work in the moments that matter is a simple idea, but it's not a small one. It changes how we work, lead and live.

Accepting you have a liability does not mean you are broken, unmotivated or underperforming. It is a sign you are doing great work. Having the awareness to see the situations that bring you undone is the realm of people pursuing results. It is an unmistakable sign you are stretching yourself for something worthwhile.

In his book *The War of Art*, Steven Pressfield makes this point very eloquently in a page titled, Resistance and Self Doubt:

"Self-doubt can be an ally. This is because it serves as an indicator of aspiration. It reflects love, love of something we dream of doing, and desire, desire to do it. If you find yourself asking yourself (and your friends), "Am I really a writer? Am I really an artist?" chances are you are. The counterfeit innovator is always wildly self-confident. The real one is scared to death."

I love this. Courageous writing that avoids success being boiled down to the simple solutions we often seek. Instead, Pressfield provides a more honest approach to achievement. When undertaking our most valuable work we experience interference, the difficulty or doubt trying to derail our effort.

Believing interference can be contained with more capability, capacity or talent, is a mistake. Success is secured when we learn to manage the interference that comes with meaningful work. Advances in neuroscience have enabled a much greater understanding of the way the brain is formed and functions. We now know interference impacts performance by how the brain is designed.

The section of the brain responsible for creating interference is the amygdala. Living at the top of the spinal column, this part of the brain is responsible for our survival and works to keep us safe. It controls the flight or fight mechanism we experience when our survival needs are at stake.

This part of the brain cares what people think because staying part of the tribe is essential to survival. Of course, survival and success are not the same things. As we look to leave our comfort zone and stretch ourselves for something worthwhile, the amygdala senses danger and is hard-wired to keep us safe. So it speaks up and tells us to sit down, stay quiet and avoid standing out.

The amygdala is the part of the brain responsible for the voice that says the timing is wrong, the budget isn't enough, the conditions aren't conducive or the system is working against you. Primed with the sole responsibility of keeping you safe, the amygdala is the source of all our interference.

The issue of course, is the work that matters, the work we care about and the work that is worth doing, involves pushing the boundaries, stepping outside what we know and are comfortable doing. The very place where the amygdala feels threatened, and prefers to stay safe, so directs our subconscious to protect the status quo.

Every time we recite the policy, work to a position description or follow someone because they are higher up the hierarchy, we are being influenced by the amygdala and acquiescing to the interference. For many people, the mere presence of interference is enough to make them surrender all hopes of success. The bad news is this biological response cannot be beaten. The good news is we can develop the capacity to understand the interference as it occurs and create structures that seduce the amygdala into feeling safe. Clearing the way for our capability to be put to work.

It's impossible to reason with interference. Just like a child throwing a tantrum in the middle of the supermarket – they can't be talked down. The parent, who makes a stand and manages the moment, can control the situation. The parent, who tries to plead, beg or bribe the child, loses control. The child knows they hold the power, which amplifies the problem. The only antidote is to take control of the situation. Negotiation is not an option. Interference is the same.

Definable Moments

The only hope you have in overcoming interference is to notice it's happening, call it out in the open and kill it with your capability. Actively deploy your skills to mitigate the problem being presented to you. Anything less and interference takes a tight hold and doesn't let go. Ever. Here are seventeen signs interference is working against you:

Change is avoided.
You are argumentative.
Saying yes is your default.
Someone else gets blamed.
You ostracize certain people.
Revenge or grudges are harbored.
You need more skills to take action.
You give solutions not ask questions.
You attend meetings that don't matter.
Patterns that don't serve you stay with you.
People or problems are addressed indirectly.
Action is delayed to wait for more information.
Procrastination and perfectionism are accepted.
Mistakes get blamed on someone or something else.
You are emotionally attached to your own perspective.
You have a list of reasons why something can't be done.
You manufacture anxiety about what will happen in the future.

If the presence of hard work was the defining factor for success, Al and Meg Donnell would never have started the Sanfilippo Children's Foundation, Rosie Batty would have never recovered and been awarded Australian of the Year; and Bethany Hamilton would never have succeeded as a professional surfer. All these people have found a way to overcome the interference.

Where is your brilliance getting beaten down?

The business idea you have had but never quite pursued. The team you could lead if you stop waiting for the title. The book idea you have waiting to be written. The boy you fancy but are too scared to approach. The money you could save if you curb your spending. The insights you could offer but are too afraid to share. The life you would love if you could commit to escaping the rut.

One of the most damaging reasons we stop doing the work we care about, is our fear of failure that something we do might not work. Of course it won't. Not all the time. Perfectionism is a sophisticated form of procrastination. Expecting you will get things right all the time, will hold you back every single time.

Tim Burton wasn't always admired in Hollywood. People thought he was dark, weird and non-conforming, so he initially struggled for his success. Some people would see this as a rejection of their art, and a clear message to stop doing the work and try something new. Tim Burton chose to do the opposite.

Firstly, he accepted people were challenged by his work, not that it was bad work. A critical distinction we all must have the courage to determine and decide. Secondly, he decided to keep pushing and working hard to publish his ideas. He knew giving in to the interference would only strengthen its resolve and make it harder to resist when it came calling again, which he knew it inevitably would.

People we see as successful have consistently achieved by learning to function with failure. They see failure as an occurrence not a behaviour trait. So when they try something and it doesn't work out, they don't default to self-criticism or believe their idea was useless or that people no longer value them.

Instead, they learn that the tactics they used and the time they used them or the person they used them on, didn't work. They make the refinements that need to be made and take a second, third or fourth action to get the job done.

The hard part of course is serving your success when interference is working so hard to divert you from your path. Like the arch nemesis in most Marvel movies, the role of interference is to create chaos, make things hard and continually test your resolve as you seek out the results that matter to you.

Definable Moments

In workshops, I often ask people to define the *real world results* they want to deliver. Not because people come with fanciful ideas that are unrealistic, but because it is essential to realise, and respect, the work we need to do occurs in the real world. Where people do judge each other, good ideas don't always get approved, conflict will arise and interference is constantly present.

Interference is like gravity. You can't see its force but can usually feel its impact. It is any negative thought, feeling or interaction you have when trying to do work that matters to you. It is the negative self-talk you experience during struggle, and the frustration you feel when other people are getting in your way. When things are working, you can be sure interference will turn up to steal the scene.

There are seven stages of interference. Each stage is designed to drain your effort, derail your progress and diminish your performance. And just like a video game with multiple stages, as you level up, things get more difficult. Knowing what they are is a helpful starting point to managing them more effectively.

STAGE 1   Personal

Like the bully in a schoolyard, interference starts by magnifying the areas of your life where you feel most uncertain, undervalued or unappreciated. Relocating your tension to someone or something else only serves its purpose because you avoid taking accountability for the outcomes you experience. Looking outside yourself for answers mitigates your most powerful weapon, the choice to take action.

STAGE 2   Obstructive

Tension obstructs you the most at the edges of your comfort zone because this is the landscape for most life-changing decisions. Interference works to keep you in your comfort zone. When you are close to achieving success, it will cast doubt on your ability. And when you are about to hit rock bottom, it will inspire you and give you hope. The point is to protect the status quo. Interference knows if you do the work and actually realise you already have what it takes to succeed, it will lose every time.

STAGE 3   Distracting

If you do start seeking out the hard work, and making an impact, interference will try and distract you. It understands the difficult work we are trying to do is a lot harder than an easier alternative. So the distraction will either be an easier alternative to the work you are currently doing, or an event that makes you question your effort and test your resolve. Either way, interference understands procrastination is a powerful ally against people who are trying to get things done.

STAGE 4   Critical

The interference you encounter comes from within. It is fuelled by your fears and when you push back, and show some fight, it attacks you personally. Your internal critic dissects your weaknesses and deepest vulnerabilities and tells you stories to sabotage your effort... You would have got that job if you were smarter. Your kids don't like you because you are never around. Really... those pants!? This is a point where tension is acute and you must be strong in order to progress.

STAGE 5   Reasoning

Having focused on fighting you, and losing so far, interference now tries to work with you by offering reasons why the work is hard to do. Many people get fooled at this point because the reasons provided are real. The deadline is tight, the lead Counsel is hard to work with and the process is confusing and causing a problem. However, what interference fails to mention, is that none of this matters. Getting the job done always involves adversity that capable people accept and overcome.

STAGE 6   Ruthless

Recognising you have the means to overcome existing difficulties, interference now recruits allies. This may be people, like you, who are battling their own interference, and so work against you to see you fail. Setting the precedent that success is possible is scary for those who still need an excuse not to do the work. So people will attack, criticise or question your motives. Stay focused on your work, avoiding self-efficacy or standing arguments that only slow you down.

DEFINABLE MOMENTS

STAGE 7   Desperate

Deep in the game now, the interference knows it is about to be beaten. It hits the panic button and prepares for one final assault, throwing the curve ball you didn't want, expect or anticipate. You need to be alert for this counter attack. With the end in sight, and success so close, you can easily fall into a false sense of security leaving yourself exposed to the final strike of interference.

PUT SKILLS TO WORK

My hope right now is that you are starting to realise the opportunity in front of you. The opportunity to pursue what matters to you, and confront the interference that will inevitably arise by putting your skills to work. Win some and learn. Lose some and learn even more. Realise your current skills have helped you but new skills will be required to reach your next level.

And quite purposefully, life manufactures these moments of tension and doubt to enable you to learn and leverage the new skills you need.

This is what people who get the job done understand intimately. The whole point of interference is to make things hard in order to prevent you from doing valuable work. But when you can see the patterns that prevent you being at your best, you give yourself the chance to make change. The alternative is to ignore what needs to change, accept the status quo, and stay stuck.

Identifying the interference and accepting the discomfort isn't easy, but it is essential for doing valuable work. Work that others choose to avoid because they prefer comfort to capability. Sales people who work the script rather than connect with the customer. Personal trainers who count out reps and keep time rather than care about client results. Leaders who avoid giving constructive feedback because of the discomfort they feel in having a difficult conversation.

The results we seek always have a defining moment. These moments are where we feel discomfort because we are doing work that exists outside our comfort zone. Work that is new, challenging, confronting or requires new capability we don't have, or didn't think we had. When we embrace the challenge, stretch our skills and achieve some success, we realise interference is not impenetrable.

At some point in a stage production, the actors have to put down their script and step into the inevitable tension that comes with learning their lines. The success you seek is the same. Accepting the discomfort means doing something that others are unlikely to do because they want safety, security or surety. The art of overcoming the interference is taking some action despite the discomfort.

Of course there are set backs, strategic misalignment, subtle changes as well as seismic shifts that scare you along the way. That's the point. Interference will always present a problem set to test your resolve for delivering the result. Or sneakily, give you an easier alternative to stop you doing the work that matters.

People who put their skills to work in the moments that matter stand out. They have a strong sense of self, a willingness to serve others, can manage competing perspectives and are rarely heard complaining. They are confident, calm, appear in control and committed to achieving the results they seek. Not some of the time, but all of the time.

This level of capability gets acquired over time by reducing your performance liability. Actively deciding to close the gap between what you think and feel, and what you do. Making the choice to invest your skills to make a positive impact is how the best get better.

2
Work worth doing

My wife is a marathon runner.

On Sunday, November 1 2009 she lined up at the start of the 40th New York marathon. Standing with the other 43,250 runners, she had trained hard that year to achieve the race qualification time and secure her place at the start.

To achieve her goal of a sub three-hour finish meant running the race at pace. With the help of her coach, she broke down the distance into split times and a diet plan to make sure her body and mind maintained their integrity to carry her to the line. Just to be sure, her sister and brother-in-law also stood on the sidelines, to provide moral support at specific points throughout the race.

Sarah ran an inspired race and crossed the finish line in 2:56:21.

For some other athletes that year, the race was a little less enjoyable. Running a race over this distance is full of moments that test the most seasoned athlete. One of the hardest is what runners often refer to as 'hitting the wall'. The period within the race, usually around the thirty-two kilometre mark, where some of the most basic functions of the body mutiny against any further movement.

Talk to a runner who has hit the wall and they will recount stories of their legs giving up beneath them, or their legs working fine but the brain suffering fatigue. Or in worse case scenarios, like Swiss athlete Gabriela Anderson-Schiess experienced at the 1984 Summer Olympics, a breakdown of the entire body system. The marathon is hard work.

Definable Moments

Not every runner hits the wall but most experience a moment during the race where they just want to stop. Finishing the marathon, as it turns out, is not just about training the body to run the forty-two kilometres without stopping. It also involves conditioning the mind to get through the moments that hurt the most, when your entire body is screaming at you to stop.

This is the moment that separates runners *wanting* to and *willing* to, and is not some mythology found solely in marathon running.

In 2007, Seth Godin published a small but insightful book about these difficult moments called *The Dip*. A highly recommended read for anyone who regularly gets stuck and feels the need to stop. The book contains a simple yet powerful model that I have adapted to reinforce the role hard work plays in performance.

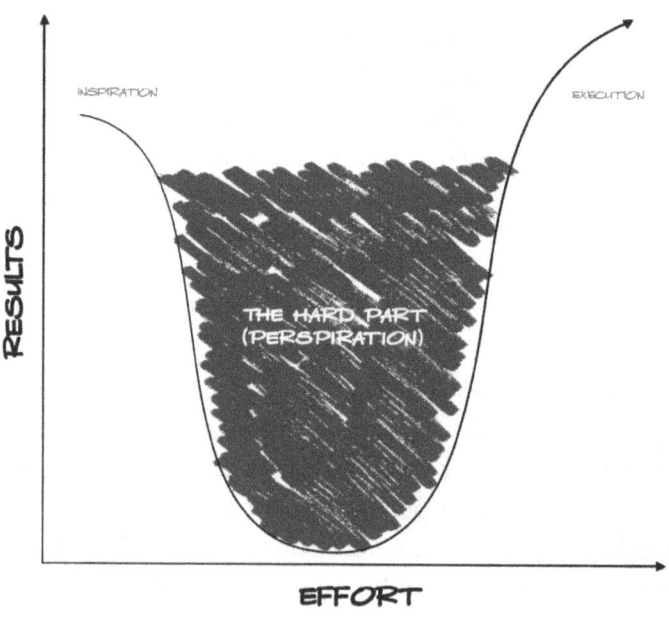

Figure 3: The Dip is the hard part between inspiration and execution.

WORK WORTH DOING

Any work worth doing has a hard part. The point in time when our aspirations for achievement get seriously challenged in some way and you feel like stopping. A point where those who achieve, despite the presence of difficulty, resist the easier alternative and do the work that delivers the desired result.

- For a parent, this is the three o'clock morning, when his child wakes up and is feeling sick, so he fights his own tiredness and tends to the child, because he wants to be a present parent.
- For a leader, it's her disengaged team demanding change but avoiding the difficult conversations, so she speaks with honesty and has a real impact, because she wants to be a leader not a manager.
- And for a project, it's the budget blowout that puts the team under pressure, so they work together and come up with a shared solution to cut costs.

The dip is the moment in any results-driven activity, when interference turns up and tries to derail your effort, so things become hard. There are three different types of dip and three different ways we try and manage them. The three *types* of dip relate to time. The ways we *manage* reinforce the impacts of the action we take.

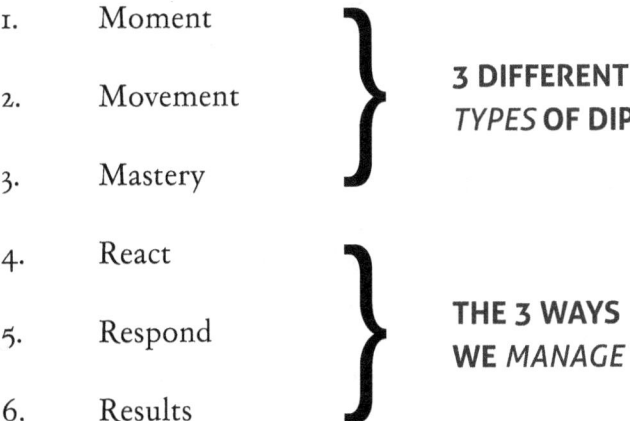

Managing the dip effectively requires an acute awareness of how you invest your energy, effort and attention when things get hard.

It is easy to burn your effort on activities you think will move you forward, only to find your frustration and fatigue actually escalate. Of the three common approaches people take to get out of the dip, only one leads to success. Therefore being aware of the different kinds of dips and appropriate approach to take is important. It will assist you diagnose what's difficult and make some decisive decisions about the action required to move you forward.

3 DIFFERENT TYPES OF DIP

1. MOMENT - perspective

Presenting to a senior Executive team I was waiting at the front of the room when the CFO came over to inform me that all the technology was down: no slides, no video, no whiteboard to use effectively, and no chance things were going to be repaired before we start. Without visual support, but wanting to make a good impression, I had a decision to make. Start to panic or show some poise.

Some dips challenge us in the moment. They come without warning and need a quick solution. These dips demand a short burst of energy, effort or focus to see the situation with the perspective of the person we want to be or the purpose we are trying to serve. Being able to make this shift in perspective is usually all it takes to move through a momentary dip, even when it feels like Armageddon.

2. MOVEMENT - progress

The Coach called me to discuss the approaching season. The players and staff were focused on success, but he knew there would be inevitable setbacks. Someone would get injured, games would be lost that should have been won, form would fluctuate and an internal issue might attract media scrutiny. Multiple dips would need to be managed to secure the Premiership. He wanted some help.

Sometimes the work we want to achieve takes time. We have a specific start and finish point, but can't predict what will happen along the way. Success is reliant on our ability to maintain momentum by seeing, and then solving, the dips that occur along the way.

Movement dips get mitigated when progress is regularly reinforced to recognise improvement, and disruptive events that occur are used to recalibrate effort to serve the desired result.

3. MASTERY - performance

Some of the most meaningful work we do involves a life-long commitment to continual improvement. We know this work never really ends because it's all about mastery. The pursuit of personal advancement that ensures continual sacrifice, stretch and sustained effort. We know working through the dips that arise is all part of being committed to our cause, whatever that may be.

For the Reverend Tim Costello, the cause is removing the negative impacts of gambling on society. Achieving this goal in his lifetime is unlikely. However, he works tirelessly for the cause to make a positive contribution. Especially when the barriers, obstacles and challenges demand the most from him. These dips are the ones when his voice, courage and commitment are required the most. A strong sense of purpose is what enables him to navigate these dips effectively.

Not all of the hard work we have to do is the same. Knowing the work that is required when confronting the different kinds of dip is essential to managing them more effectively. However, even with that knowledge, turning knowledge into action, when you find yourself in the dip, can be riddled with challenge.

So it is equally important to understand the different ways to manage the dip and the impacts each of these have in advancing your success.

THE 3 WAYS WE MANAGE

1. REACT - emotion

When we come across circumstances that push, challenge or confront us, we can react emotionally rather than respond effectively. We stop doing the work and avoid the positive push that is often required to deliver advanced results. This reactive response protects our emotions because we retreat from the work we need to be doing. We avoid a fear of failure by creating a false fall-back position.

This approach was glaringly evident to me when undertaking some work with a talented track athlete. She was a consistent podium finisher at State level, however rarely finished first having consistently been beaten by her rival. Consultation with her Coach, and conversations with her to discuss the issue, clearly showed her issue was not technical or physical. She was in great shape and getting high performance coaching and training. Her issue, like so many top performing athletes, was a matter of overcoming her mindset interference.

Watching her run over the course of four different meets, against a variety of opponents, showed a distinct pattern. She prepared well. Warmed up the same way each time and invariably got a good start. She consistently ran well and put herself in a position to win, but she never did win. Not one race.

The issue was in her finish. When the final surge came, and each competitor was pushing hard for a place, she didn't respond. She avoided the fight at the finish. She was subconsciously giving herself a false fall-back position. Holding back on her effort meant there was always an excuse for not quite achieving. She didn't have to confront the reality that she gave everything she had but didn't finish first.

2. RESPOND - capability

Results we seek can get hijacked when we solve the problems caused by the dip with existing capability, position or preferences. Experience that, while serving us well, can also restrict us from seeing repetitive patterns of behaviour that no longer serve our best interests. Default decision-making often causes us to stop when we really should stick, and stick when we really should stop.

A friend of mine is on his fourth marriage. He is successful in most areas of his life. His holds a senior position at his work, his friendship network is strong, he coaches a junior sport team and takes regular holidays to manage his stress. However, when it comes to his relationships, he has a major blind spot that has formed a pattern of behaviour that impacts his ability to keep a partner.

He meets someone and everything starts off beautifully. She is interesting, vivacious, independent and attractive. Life is good, the relationship gets more serious and so they decide to move in together and eventually, marry.

This is where he feels the relationship change. The mundane now has to get managed, the day-to-day details need to be discussed, the clothes need to be washed and house needs to be cleaned. The beautiful date nights and personal appreciation of each other doesn't have to end however this is the world he prefers to inhabit and is his blind spot. The perfect relationship, where every day is carefree, super coordinated and cleaned for you, doesn't exist.

So rather than develop his capability and capacity to create a remarkable relationship that manages the routine, he quits and starts all over again. He stops when he really could stick and work to achieve the remarkable relationship he is genuinely trying to find. His approach is flawed.

Before you judge my friend too quickly, there are numerous examples of how the response approach influences certain structures or decisions in daily life:

1. Health clubs over-subscribe memberships knowing some who join, will also experience the dip of not seeing results fast enough, so stop coming. The clubs capitalise by selling more memberships than the actual floor space allows. They know some members who sign up, will stop rather than stick.

2. In a cubicle or office somewhere near you there is a person who hates their job. The love they once had for what they do, has died. So they turn up, do the bare minimum and go home feeling largely unsatisfied. Why? Because it's much easier to stay in a job you hate, than go through the challenging process of finding new employment. They stick rather than stop.

3. What about you? What's that nagging problem that keeps coming up for you throughout your personal or professional life? The thing that no matter what you do, or think you have addressed,

continues to get in your way. Have you stopped when you really should stick? Or stuck when you really should stop?

3. RESULTS - purpose

The key to escaping the dips you find yourself facing is to have a strong sense of purpose and take the specific actions that deliver the future you desire. This is easier said than done because it takes courage and commitment. You must make the choice to avoid whining about what's wrong, or waiting to be told what to do, embracing the authority you have, to do what matters to you.

Remember, working through a dip can take a moment or a lifetime. Successful examples can range from a simple event, to something life changing. Seeing a receptionist calm an irate customer is getting through the dip. So is the senior leader who makes a stand against inappropriate behaviour. People who learn a new language also learn how to navigate the dip. You can learn too.

The dip is frustrating, confusing and can often be overwhelming. Seeing clearly, amidst all the complexity, is essential for navigating the dip successfully. It can be hard to know whether we should stick or stop. Sometimes we make a change only to find the reality we face is the same. The grass isn't any greener. So before making any meaningful decisions when you're in a dip, ask yourself:

If I invest myself and do the hard work to get through this dip, will I succeed?

If the answer is yes, then stick and do the hard work that will yield a positive result. If the answer is no, stop and reinvest your effort in work that will make more of an impact. The question helps you to decide what matters, define the work that is worth doing, and then focus your energy on getting *that* done.

Hard work has always been the baseline for achievement because the results we seek take incredible amounts of time, energy and focus. Rather than fight it, we have to roll up our sleeves and get on with it. This is what interference hates the most – people who understand the hard work and choose to invest their skills to get through the dip. Doing this valuable work is what makes results happen and as a consequence is the work that forges a fantastic reputation.

DO VALUABLE WORK

The hard work is difficult to do when the day-to-day drift becomes a full-time role. Competing deadlines, busy schedules, demanding clients or the difficult situations that demand your time and keep you busy. Mistaking this productive work for performance work can often keep you time poor and task fatigued.

You'll know what I mean if you have ever felt like one of those plate spinners at the circus. Rushing around, doing the best with what you have and working hard to get things done, feeling like the balance between success and sanity is some kind of elusive deal. Getting stuck in busy prevents us building a better future.

This is made even more difficult by our current culture promoting the idea of the workaholic. Where busyness seems to be subconsciously connected to our level of capability and value. We boast about how many emails we have, how little time we have, how much work we need to do, or how we are dragged from pillar to post every weekend to keep up with the kid's commitments.

In their book *Rework*, Jason Fried and David Heinemeier Hansson highlight the flawed thinking of people who wear being busy as a badge of honour:

Working more doesn't mean you care more or get more done. It just means you work more. Workaholics make the people who don't stay late feel inadequate for working reasonable hours. That leads to guilt and poor morale all around.

It leads to an ass-in-seat mentality - people stay late out of obligation, even if they aren't really being productive. Workaholics aren't heroes. They don't save the day – they just use it up. The real hero is already home because she figured out a faster way to get things done.

Definable Moments

Undertaking hours of work that has little or no resemblance to what matters to you, or motivates you, destroys the soul. We've all been there at some point in our work careers when someone at a social function asks: "What do you do?" And instead of lighting up, we wind up our internal PR agent and give a pitch to convince a complete stranger we have a good job and do a good job.

When we are doing the work that matters this conversation changes. We revel in the opportunity to share the project we are working on, the challenge we are undertaking, the performance we are seeking or people we are impacting. We naturally transition from PR agent to our passionate and authentic selves.

Defining the difficult moments that arise is the ultimate form of valuable work. The distinguished work that gets you through the dip and drives you forward. Work that is impossible to give focus to if you feel constantly overworked and overwhelmed.

How do you do less mundane work and focus on the work that is meaningful and matters? You start by understanding the four forms of work you choose to do, review the work you are currently doing, and assess the spread of work for the meaningful opportunities that advance results and enhance your reputation.

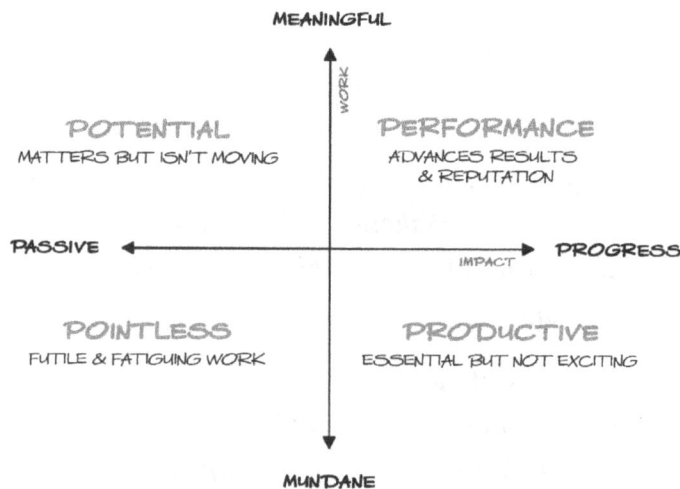

Figure 4: A positive reputation starts by managing four forms of work.

Pointless work involves the actions we are taking, or not taking, that keep us stuck in situations we don't enjoy. This work usually involves issues that cause frustration and fatigue and where inaction is contributing to the problem. This quadrant drains our energy and wastes our time. Spending time doing this work is the very definition of pointless. So here are three ways to avoid it:

1. **Stop doing**

   Lawyers send a cease and desist letter when they want someone to stop doing something. Take a similar approach by committing to enforce a cease and desist with your pointless work. You will soon find out if anyone cares. Including you.

2. **Clarify value**

   This work is often labeled as pointless because we don't see the value. Gaining clarity as to how this work serves the bigger picture can change the context of this work. Seek out explanations to give the pointless a point.

3. **Minimum standards**

   If you can't stop doing this work, but can see the value in it, find a way to get it done at the minimum acceptable standard. Dedicating your time to do this work brilliantly not only wastes your time, it also reduces the energy and effort you need for the more valuable work.

Productive work is the essential and often unexciting work that keeps us moving forward. The set and forget tasks essential for being successful. This is the work that is important to *maintain performance*. Busyness occurs when these tasks get too much of our attention. They take your time rather than give you time.

High performers hack their productivity to prevent busyness. They are adept at seeing regular patterns and streamlining how this productive work gets done. This means finding more feasible alternatives for doing the day-to-day jobs by diminishing it, delegating it or doing it more effectively.

1. **Enhance efficiency**

    Many of the jobs we have to do every day are repetitive, mundane or set and forget tasks that don't deserve a lot of thought or attention. Making these tasks faster, easier, or more efficient, gets this work done as quickly and efficiently as possible. This frees up precious time to focus on higher value work.

    If you are one of the reported 78% of people who complain about the avalanche of email, this will resonate with you. Taming your inbox overflow by applying some simple rules around your email management is a simple tactic that will enhance your email efficiency*. Taking this step will free up your time, energy and personal productivity that can be reinvested in more valuable work.

    * Impossible of course if you are one of those people who take pride in telling others how many emails you have as proof of your importance, worth and value.

2. **Delegate detail**

    A client of mine is a guru around personal productivity. She follows some simple rules and encourages her team to do the same. Delegation is one of them. She once said to me: "Andrew, I will never let go of strategy but will always let go of activity." Brilliant. Capable people rarely get caught up in controlling activity.

    Micromanaging what people do because you don't trust them, like them or think they are as good as you, is tiring and even worse when you try it out, get disappointed, and take the work back rather than create improved clarity. The need for constant control is what keeps us time poor and task fatigued.

3. **Embrace adequacy**

    Our bias for high achievement can often mean we overwork, and overdeliver on the tasks that don't require that level of dedication. The price is having less time, energy, and effort for the opportunities that deliver greater impact and accelerate our influence. Adequacy is knowing when good is good enough.

Professional services firms understand this implicitly. They segment their clients based on the value they bring to the business, not just via income, but client referrals, work volumes or social influence. Segmentation embraces adequacy as a philosophy because Bronze members receive the good enough service, so that time, energy and effort can be directed to pleasing the Platinum clientele.

Potential work is often where you can identify and address your performance liability. This is often the hard work we need to be doing, but are avoiding. Or is the work we are actively undertaking but it is not having the influence or impact we desire, so we stagnate. Before resigning to the status quo, and experiencing further frustration, consider trying one of these three strategies:

1. Work undercover

Sometimes life can work against us. Rather than seek permission, get on with doing the work that matters to you and makes sense to you. If you make a start and see it is working because others are interested, engaged or appreciative of what you are doing, your actions become the catalyst for creating change.

Definable Moments was a hard book to write. With a business to run, a newborn baby just arrived home, and a frenetic fifteen-month-old already at home, time was relatively scarce. So I did some work undercover. I dedicated two evenings a week to turn off the TV and work in the front room away from distractions. The result is the book you are reading now, whilst maintaining a healthy home life and marriage.

2. Reframe results

Work that is *personal* often matters to you. Work that is *purposeful* matters to many people. Finding a way to reframe your work to support the broader strategy is essential for having influence and impact. This starts with getting savvy about the strategic priorities of your key stakeholders.

The hardest part of achieving alignment is accepting the responsibility to do the work. Accepting that different perspectives are part of advancing performance and need to be influenced, not overcome. Seeing how your individual position can serve a shared purpose will shift work from stagnant to successful.

3. Practise elsewhere

If you have made a genuine attempt at some of these strategies without success, maybe it's time to accept the work you want to do can't be done in your current setting. If this is the case, there are three feasible alternatives. Pursue the work in your personal time, transfer to someone who will support what you do, or in the most extreme circumstances, leave and go elsewhere.

Performance work is the highly valuable work that is difficult to do, but delivers incredible momentum when we move it forward. Seeking out and spending time doing this work builds confidence, capability and the capacity to get things done. People working in this quadrant successfully rely on autonomy, resilience and collaboration to get things done. This is how they stay there:

1. Manage energy

People who perform worry less about time management and more about energy management. They know being engaged and energised enables two weeks work to be done in twenty-four hours. The high performing people we admire aren't superhuman. They're supremely astute at managing their fitness, food and focus to maintain high levels of performance throughout the day.

Here are five guiding principles for maintaining high performance:

1 - 2	Breaks every 90 minutes
2 - 3	Exercise sessions each week
4 - 5	Glasses of water through the day
6 - 7	Meals per day to maintain your energy
8 - 9	Hours of sleep every night for adequate rest

WORK WORTH DOING

2. **Understand currency**

   One of the ways we get paid for the work we do is through our salary. The cash deposit that reaches your account every fortnight or month. However, there is an alternate currency that high performers learn to leverage. The currency that gets people motivated to do what they do. Wanting to make a difference, gain a promotion, get home on time, work autonomously or be valued for their work.

   Working on purpose means you receive your alternate currency. You get into what you do because you are motivated by what you do. Doing performance-orientated work is much easier if you are aligned to your highest purpose and are empowered to succeed. How much alternate currency are you receiving?

4. **Contextual clarity**

   Performance works best when people can see with contextual clarity. The ability to think strategically, but deliver operationally, so work gets done. This duality involves the ability to see the world through a wide Google Earth view, as well as detailed street level view, zooming in or out as required to get work done.

   Having trouble with a colleague? Zoom in and see what's going on to recalibrate the relationship. Asked to give a presentation to the Board? Zoom out and assess trends impacting the market, customers or competitive landscape. This duality is difficult, but a core capability for people who can get the job done.

These suggestions are not a panacea for every performance challenge you face in managing the demands of a day. Rather, they are provided as a set of helpful reminders about what you could leverage, or be lacking, when finding yourself doing work that doesn't align to your purpose, priorities or personality.

Taking proactive steps to focus on performance-orientated work is magical for motivation. Drift gets replaced with drive, enabling more work to be done in less time. Productivity peaks, engagement increases and performance rapidly accelerates as you do the work that matters to you and makes sense to you.

Making the transition from doing what someone else says, to delivering work that motivates you and matters to you, is difficult. Especially when the systems, structures and senior leaders of many organisations are still operating with old management models not equipped to motivate a modern workforce. Equally true for family and friends who encourage safety, rather than our success.

There are many ways we self-sabotage our future. We wait for instructions rather than work things out ourselves. We choose safety over the chance to step up. We appoint blame instead of addressing the deficit of our decisions. We avoid facing fear, doubt and detractors limiting our ability to really learn. This used to be tolerated when the world was largely stable and predictable.

But the world of work has changed.

THE FUTURE OF WORK

As we mature into the new global economy, the lines that define people and performance have become quite blurred. In the past, the critical positions were seen as roles on the org chart. The CEO was more important than the CFO who was more important than the person at reception making the first impression.

This used to be true when work consisted of regular, routine and repetitive tasks. When people turned up, did their job to the best of their ability, and went home. But in the new economy of connection and attention, change is constant, work is complex and competition is fierce. The critical roles are shifting to the people with the courage to put their capability to work and get the job done.

Thornton May, the American futurist, correctly asserts that we have reached the end of attendance based compensation (ABC). This was where people completed a set of prescribed tasks in return for a salary, and did what the boss wanted to achieve promotion and protection. Anyone can be trained to turn up and follow orders. But people, who turn up to work and passively follow orders, kill performance.

Work worth doing

To understand the principles of modern day performance, let's explore the two different types of work, and delve a little deeper into how work has changed.

Work we do can be divided into two main categories – algorithmic and heuristic. Algorithmic work describes the less complex tasks that need to be done, those that require little thought or judgment. Like completing the end of month billings, timesheets, greeting a customer or attending the monthly meeting. Algorithmic work also includes roles where people do pretty much the same thing over and over in the same way. Think car park attendant and you are getting the picture.

Heuristic work is the opposite. There is no set formula, predetermined path or one way to succeed. The work is often unknown, undefined, ambiguous and challenging. We must experiment with possibilities and discover a way forward that best works for us personally. This means thinking laterally, leveraging capability and overcoming any obstacles that arise along the way.

Making the distinction between the different types of work is important because it highlights how work has changed. Initially, during the twentieth century, the majority of work was algorithmic. And not just in the factories standing on the assembly line. Even when blue collars got traded for white, work was largely routine. The drill press became the keyboard, the assembly line became the meeting and the spec sheet became our KPIs. Work largely remained planned, controlled and measured.

But today, work is evolving at a rapid rate. The algorithmic work we once did is being automated, outsourced or outdated. What this means for anyone doing routine work, whether you are an accountant, lawyer, computer programmer or consultant, is you are in danger of being replaced by a robot, cheaper labour living overseas or the software system that is more efficient and cost effective.

With the menial and mundane work becoming more redundant, the complex and creative work is now driving competitive advantage, the heuristic work that requires thinking, personal judgment and decision-making. Entire industries like print, music and manufacturing, are already feeling the impacts of this change. It is not something that is coming. It is something that is already happening.

Maintaining the work that is rigid and restrictive discourages people to use their insight and intellect to succeed. This exact dilemma has created an issue for the forward thinking leaders in the automotive industry. Dealer Principles who are aware of this limitation are looking for a different approach to the tired and traditional 'Road to a Sale' that has dominated the industry for decades.

The Road to a Sale is a ten-step process to help sales people assess a customer's needs, build rapport and highlight the features and benefits of a specific vehicle. It purposefully plans out precise steps to greet a customer, manufacture positive emotions, manage their objections and ultimately secure their commitment and accept the sale. All people have to do is know the steps.

Prior to the Internet, the Road to a Sale methodology was a powerful and profitable way to sell cars. Primarily because the approach preyed upon a lack of pricing transparency, and slick sales tactics that were once prevalent within the industry, and maybe still are, but the Internet is changing everything.

Now, buyers are much more informed about the vehicle they are purchasing before they even enter the dealership. They are less willing to follow steps in a process when the price, specifications, stock options and special deals have already been posted and promoted online. Customers are much more savvy, so the Road to a Sale methodology no longer serves as a process of purchase. The work of a sales person has moved from algorithmic to more heuristic work.

The sales teams who have adapted to this change, and taken the time to connect with someone authentically, remain a rarity within the industry. Paying for them is possible. Building a team of them will create competitive advantage. And this is the challenge confronting any leader, in any business or industry, responsible for delivering results. Knowing how to motivate not just mandate performance.

Work worth doing

The modern manifesto for changing the way we get work done that should be on the reading list of every forward thinking leader, is *Drive* by Daniel Pink:

Most of us believe that the best way to motivate others and ourselves is with external rewards like money. That's a mistake. The secret to performance and satisfaction – at work, at school, and at home – is the deeply human need to direct our own lives, to learn, to create new things, and to do better by ourselves, and our world.

There are four decades of research that exposes the mismatch between what science knows and what business does – and how that affects every aspect of life. The three essential elements to motivation – autonomy, mastery and purpose – are critical to change how we think and transform how we live.

Many organisations haven't made this shift. They are still working from the premise that work gets done by mandating certain time, tasks and desired behaviours, rather than motivating people to do the work that matters. The premise of this approach is to pay people properly and monitor them closely. But we now know people need to be engaged, empowered and motivated. And the structures we once used to motivate people for routine work don't work so well for the creative, collaborative and non-formulaic work of the future.

Similarly, we haven't made this shift. We wait for instructions rather than work things out ourselves. We choose safety over the chance to step up. We avoid facing our own fear, doubt and detractors limiting our leverage. We stay in jobs, relationships and lifestyle choices that no longer serve us because it's safe, and spend our days wishing or willing things to be different.

The way we manage people to achieve high performance has taken a seismic shift. That is why Chapter 6 has been dedicated entirely to exploring how leaders can master motivation by making work **work**. However, the starting context for this conversation must be reinforcing the importance of our own responsibility.

DEFINABLE MOMENTS

One day Bernie Hawker had had enough.

She stood up, started a conversation and became a champion for change. She didn't quit her job, or gain a new title or ask for more money. She just started doing her job in a different way. She saw a decline in the results of her school's largely disadvantaged students and wanted to instigate some improvement.

Bernie got inspired.

She started looking at how she could improve the literacy results at her school. She started a Professional Learning Community (PLC). A group of volunteer teachers committed to increase their skills to teach writing – regardless of their subject area. The group met fortnightly, after school hours, to collaborate and construct a comprehensive suite of unique writing tools for students and teachers to use in the classroom. And use them they did.

The literacy placemats and writing arrows they developed enabled targeted teaching of specific writing skills. This enabled teachers to tailor specific skill development for specific groups of students. Separating the different writing levels gave students a strong focus, and sense of progress, which has seen the school consistently produce above average results within their region.

The PLC now has over twenty people, almost half the teaching staff, turning up every fortnight to work out ways to improve student learning. Teachers are collaborating, student's confidence is growing, and professional coaching and sharing continues to encourage pedagogical best practice at the school.

You probably haven't heard of Bernie. She isn't famous, can't demand a private audience with the Dali Lama, or even persuade her children to keep their rooms clean. She didn't ask for permission to do her job any better, she just made the choice. Bernie is an ordinary person who made a conscious choice to do extraordinary work.

If she can do it, so can you.

Here's the caveat. If you want a job where you avoid responsibility to escape accountability, then don't complain when the boss keeps telling you what to do. And if you are the leader who is unable, or unwilling, to empower your people, get used to micro-managing the mundane and loathing Monday mornings.

And here's the rub. If you find a job you love, seek out opportunities to succeed, take some calculated risks and get comfortable with the occasional failure, don't be surprised if you accelerate your results and advance your reputation. Where people seek you out for your opinions, insights and intellect to get the work done.

Getting the job done is hard work. And that is a good thing. If the results you want to achieve were easy there would be no value. Give anyone the right knowledge, conditions, timeframe or budget and they will perform. But so would everyone else. There would be no value. And the future of work is all about value. Delivering in moments that matter by doing work that matters.

HARD CREATES VALUE

People who get the job done make the decision to move beyond their position description, or personal preference, to do work that is valuable. They turn up, tune in to what needs to be done, and consistently do the difficult work that makes a difference, moves things forward and makes results happen.

Charlie Teo is a world-class surgeon who operates on brain tumors when other doctors have told patients there are no more options. When other doctors have decided the risks are too great to operate, Charlie sees the value in trying to save a life. For people who have a brain tumor, and have been told there is no hope, Charlie Teo is precisely the person you want holding the scalpel.

He operates and has a reasonable rate of success. For people who have been given a diagnosis of incurable brain cancer, he provides an alternative for life. Thankfully, I am unaware of Dr Teo's consulting fees, but I suspect they are large. They can afford to be, because when it comes to saving the life of a person facing death, the price tag becomes irrelevant. The possibility of a cure far outweighs the cost of his service. This makes Charlie Teo valuable. Delivering value isn't exclusive to high-end professions either.

Frank Carbone, a tram driver on my route, is enthusiastic. He announces each stop, waits for the elderly passengers to sit down before he departs, and always greets people as they enter his tram. Sure, he could just be a tram driver who sits in a protective booth, oblivious to passengers and bored by following tracks that predetermine his direction. But he isn't. He delights customers. This makes Frank Carbone valuable.

Compare Frank's approach to people who are stuck in the old way of work. The waiter who takes your order and delivers your food, the sales person who only wants to secure the deal, or the doctor who sees patients rather than serves people. Failing to see the value of your work, or doing the bare minimum wanting the world to change while you stay the same, will only lead to failure.

Maybe this all sounds quite unreasonable. It's unreasonable to go the extra mile for a boss who doesn't care. It's unreasonable to question the client when they pay the bill. It's unreasonable to take the lead if you don't lead the team. And it's unreasonable to question authority if you believe you need their approval. Fortunately, there are unreasonable people doing the valuable work and making a difference. Unfortunately, you now have to compete with them.

MAKING A START

Doing valuable work doesn't mean turning up tomorrow and making a career changing decision, or taking a large leap of faith without first considering the implications. It means finding things you can do that will get you started.

If you usually feel stress what would it take to find calmness? If you are being unproductive how could you better manage your time? If your team is facing a problem what insight or action could help move that issue forward? If you can do this once, then of course you can do it again. And that's the point.

We all have historical moments of courage. Whether they occurred last decade, last year or last week, something happened, and you immediately felt fear and anxiety arise. Probably manifesting in your head with a voice telling you to stop, step back and avoid the risk in front of you. But for some reason, you saw the opportunity in front of you and decided to step forward. That was the moment you deployed the biggest, boldest and best version of yourself.

Finding the courage to deploy your capability in these difficult moments is what gets you through the dip. When part of you wants to step back, play it safe and do what you have always done, but instead, the courageous part of you speaks up, encourages you to take the path less trodden, and make a difference.

Let me share three suggestions that might be helpful as you decide to dedicate your capability to define a definable moment:

1. ASSESS THE RISK

When you next find yourself at the crossroad of stepping up or shrinking back, assess the risks. Every choice we make has prizes and punishments. Often, we restrict what is possible by overstating the risks. We see them adversely, in absolutes, or ending up as anarchy. We can also lose sight of rewards to be gained and so default to safety. Be clear about the risks and rewards to accurately assess the course of action that best serves your future.

2. TAKE ACTION

Taking action doesn't have to mean pushing all your chips into the middle of the table and going 'all in' This all or nothing approach is what can terrify some people into inaction by amplifying the negative consequences we fear when something doesn't quite happen the way we intended. Sometimes the small cautionary step, or series of steps, is a more appropriate way to trial your approach, test out the waters and turn inaction into action.

One exception. If *you decide* the reward is worth a big risk, then go big. Don't be half-hearted.

3. REPLACE PERFECTION

The last thing to do is review your success. When we set about getting something done that matters to us, we hope for the best. The reality is most success occurs as a series of steps and involves a stumble or two along the way. Replace perfection with progress and leave yourself open to a second, third or fourth step. This will give you a more realistic perspective of the work to be done at the start and delight you if your success experiences the fast track.

Work that is worth doing involves set backs, strategic misalignment, subtle changes or seismic shifts that scare people along the way. The moments that occur in the dip can derail the most seasoned performer. Rather than ignore or be interrupted by them, you must identify and positively impact them. This is how high performing people do the work that matters and get the job done.

3
Success has structure

Early in my career I was working at a not-for-profit agency. A year into the job I was asked to meet privately with the Chairman of the Board. There had been some financial inconsistencies in the monthly reports that I had legitimately raised as part of the monthly meetings, leading to some vigorous debate.

The Chair was displeased and requested a private conversation. Walking into his city apartment, I quickly realised we weren't going to be meeting alone. Sitting on the lounge sipping their coffee was the Company's lead Counsel. My stomach did a somersault as I immediately felt my loyalty, and future career, were about to come into question.

Over a course of coffee, and croissants that nobody ate, we debated the issue concerning the financial irregularities for three hours. Despite a list of prevailing reasons being offered, accepting 'creative accounting' to conceal some serious concerns in the business was not something I was willing to overlook as a Board member. We were at an impasse.

That's when the CEO slid two pieces of paper across the table in front of me. He turned them over and briefly explained that having reached an impasse there was a decision to be made. Turning over the first page, he explained I could choose to accept and endorse the majority decision of the Board. sign the piece of paper detailing that fact and that would be the end of the matter.

Or, he said, I could sign the other piece of paper. Turning over the document confirmed my suspicions. Resign now. Effective immediately.

DEFINABLE MOMENTS

TENSION SEEKS RESOLUTION

The definable moments we encounter are not always this dramatic, but do involve some tension. The tension created by a discrepancy between where we are, and where we want to be. This includes a feeling of discomfort, difficulty or opportunity that primes our flight or fight response, our internal mechanism that makes results happen because we know that tension always seeks resolution.

This becomes really interesting when you look at the table below and realise how often the tension resolution dynamic is occurring in everything that we do:

Tension	Resolution
Asking a question...	...invites an answer
Your body feels thirsty...	...so you grab a drink
You have a business idea...	...so start your own venture
Movies play scary music...	...before the serial killer strikes
You are running late...	...so you drive through an amber light

This structure of tension and resolution occurs hundreds of times a day and is the reason we take action. We feel overweight – so we start the diet. We are nervous about presenting – so do some preparation. The house has become untidy – so we start to clean. We have a spare five minutes – so reach for our smartphone. We want to buy a house – so start a savings plan.

All of our efforts for achieving success are underpinned by this dynamic of tension and resolution. The performance tension that drives our aspiration, ambition and desire. And the preventative tension that derails effort by using fear, distraction and doubt. Each type of tension promotes a preferred tendency for movement, and as we make decisions, the tension dynamic changes.

Having the ability to identify this tension dynamic, and know how to manage it effectively, is essential when trying to accelerate your success. Imagine you are alone in a room. This room represents one thing you are trying to positively achieve right now.

SUCCESS HAS STRUCTURE

While you may have multiple choices, try to focus on just one. It could be learning piano, enhancing your influence, building your business, working with a difficult client or speaking fluent Spanish.

Now imagine that around your waist there are two large rubber bands. One of these rubber bands stretches from your waist and is tethered to the wall behind you. That is your **current reality** or where you are right now. The other rubber band stretches from around your waist to the wall in front of you. This is your desired **future state** or where you want to be. (This picture may help.)

Think about what happens as you start to move from your current reality to your desired future state. The current reality band begins to tighten and you feel **preventative tension** trying to pull you back to where you started. As you step towards what you want, the tension becomes greater, and so the work becomes harder. This is because the primary role of preventative tension is to protect the status quo and prevent any forward movement.

In the absence of **performance tension** being present, the easiest action to take to reduce the tension being felt is to move back towards your current reality.

So this is what you do. And as you ease the tension being felt by moving back toward your current reality, there is another change in the structural dynamic.

DEFINABLE MOMENTS

The future state band begins to tighten and you feel performance tension trying to pull you towards where you want to be. The more you move away from your future state, the positive tension associated with aspiration and ambition start to inspire you about the success you desire. This is because the primary role of performance tension is to harness your energy and effort for achievement.

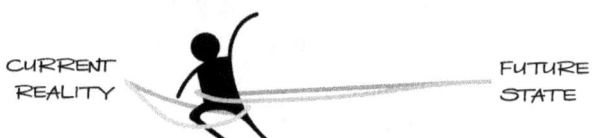

Can you see how this oscillation occurs in the task you are currently thinking about positively impacting? The continual back and forth dynamic can be frustrating. We oscillate from periods of energy and effort, to frustration and fatigue, as we work hard doing the best we can with the resources we have, only to feel, despite our best efforts, that success is some kind of elusive deal.

Like many other books, *Definable Moments* had five near death experiences during the writing phase. Times where the book stalled as I sat on the couch and asked my wife whether it was a good idea or would it resonate with the intended audience or, in my darkest days, whether the writing was actually any good. As a true source of performance tension, she rallied my composure and confidence.

Equally, there were positive and productive days where the writing would flow and I felt fantastic. At some stage during the morning however, preventative tension would arrive attempting to derail the progress being made. Swimming in the middle of the day, long coffee breaks or sitting on the front steps enjoying the sun were often the ways I managed to subconsciously sabotage my success.

Doing the work that matters to get the job done means we must recognise the two tensions at play, and resolve any tension towards our desired future state. Making the choice to resolve the tension forward will dramatically impact the level of success you experience in your personal and professional life.

SUCCESS HAS STRUCTURE

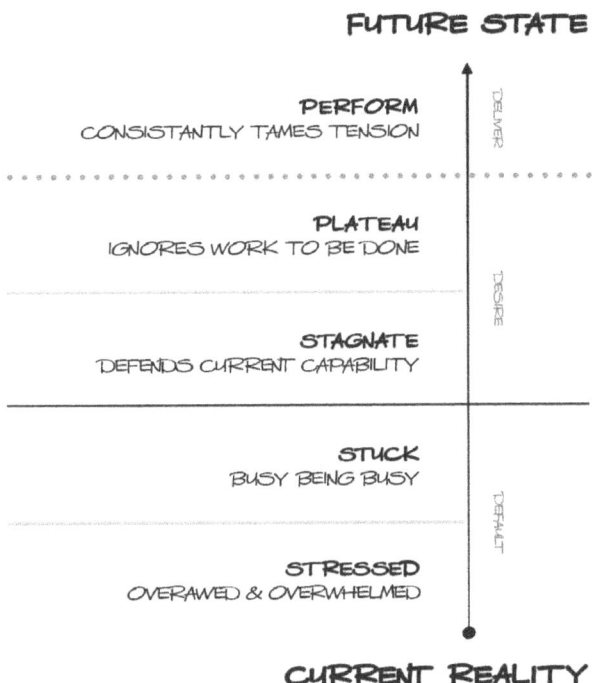

Figure 8: Levels of performance arising from how tension is resolved.

This model reflects the different levels of success we experience depending on how the inevitable tension associated with doing the work that matters gets resolved. Essentially, whether the tension gets relieved backwards, reinforcing your current reality, or resolved forward, to deliver your desired future state.

Let's explore each of the levels in a bit more detail.

SURVIVAL
Operating under stress
Losing a large client that puts profits under pressure, being overlooked for promotion or suffering a serious setback can lead to stress and a serious loss of perspective. When operating under significant stress we work below the line of performance or productivity. We default strictly to survival.

Definable Moments

STUCK
Burdened by busyness
We can often use busyness as a badge of honour believing the busier we are, the more important and valuable we appear. The truth is, most busy people are consumed by the day-to-day drift and find it hard to escape the demands being placed upon them. Demands that often serve someone else's needs.

As a consequence, times of tension are rarely predicted, and when they arise, are seen as problems to be solved. Focusing on solving problems, not seeking a sustainable solution, can keep us stuck. Working hard on the wrong thing makes us feel time poor, task fatigued and burdened by a state of busyness.

STAGNATE
Defends current capability
Have you ever gone to someone for advice about a presenting issue only to find yourself reinforcing your current reality to them, justifying why things can't be done? This is the classic mistake of people who stagnate.

Rather than accept the stretch to think differently, try something new or accept a personal insight, we get stuck defending our position or preferences. We develop personal propaganda around our own perspective to avoid the painful reality we are unwilling to confront. That something isn't working, a new approach is needed and we are the person responsible for the result.

PLATEAU
Ignores work to be done
Experiencing a plateau is often the result of us dreaming and not doing. The book we are going to write, the business we are going to start, the client we really want to work with, or the planning offsite that initially excites people, but eventually ends up as a fossil in the filing cabinet.

When a strong sense of where you want to go is met with equally strong avoidance of seeing where you are, you plateau. Avoiding the current reality creates a personal blind spot to the hard, difficult and demanding work that needs to be done. As a consequence, aspirations remain ideas without action.

PERFORM
Consistently tames tension

When we perform through tension we are using our ability to adeptly see the current reality *and* desired future state with equal accuracy. This can be very hard to do when a customer is complaining, a colleague is being underhanded or forces outside of your control suddenly make things difficult for you.

Being able to manage this tensional duality is difficult, but forms the major difference between those who desire success, and those who deliver it. They have the ability to see the current reality, but actively choose to take positive actions that resolve any prevailing tension towards the desired future state.

Actor Jim Carrey once said: "The problem with life is there is no danger music". There is no dramatic score to our lives that makes us aware something serious is about to happen. But he's wrong. Experiencing tension *is* life's danger music letting us know we are in a moment that matters. The tension highlights our opportunity for action that we choose to ignore, or positively impact, by putting our skills to work to resolve the tension towards the future you desire.

This doesn't mean leaping forth to solve the biggest, scariest or most significant change that is confronting you right now. The skill of being able to see and solve tension positively can commence with small, seemingly insignificant decisions. Here are some recent decisions I've made to illustrate the point:

- Calling a client to say I am running late rather than feel anxious
- Challenging an Executive team on their commitment for change
- Heading out for a run to be healthy despite feeling tired from the day
- Reflecting on my contribution to a problem before blaming someone else
- Being present when playing with my kids rather than worrying about work

Making these small decisions is less about succeeding and more about learning. Learning to perform rather than succumb to panic. Learning to feel your fear rather than work to avoid it. Learning to back your ability rather than question your authority. Learning to rally your choices rather than restrict your options. Learning to deal with being wrong as you fail forward to eventually be right.

Of course, this is easier said than done because the pull of preventative tension is strong, and the reality is we don't always have the motivation to move the tension forward. When things get hard, or we occasionally get derailed, we can fall into the false belief that the situation is hopeless or we are helpless. But this just isn't the case.

EFFORT ISN'T EFFORTLESS

We only have a finite amount of time and energy to invest in what matter to us. Yes, we can sustain some super human effort for a short period when we need to finish a major project, nurse a sick child in the middle of the night or conquer the approaching crisis, but it is not a state we can sustain forever.

We don't have an endless supply of energy.

Energy operates like a bank balance. You start the day with a certain energy balance in your account. As you go about engaging in the activities during the day, you spend energy from your account. Issues that require more intense or difficult effort demand more energy. The more exertion we expend, the faster we diminish our account. When our account is low it needs to be replenished.

This process of energy depletion is called cognitive fatigue. This is when performance declines as cognitive tasks are undertaken over an extended period of time. Dr Clare McMahon, a senior lecturer in the Department of Biomedical and Health Sciences at Swinburne University, used athletes to explore how cognitive fatigue affects performance. Working with two German colleagues, twenty athletes were strapped to some sophisticated machines that measured and monitored their performance, then ran a three-kilometre time trial. Twice.

The first time, athletes followed their usual pre-race routine of a short warm up and stretching prior to commencing their run. For consistency, researchers set a prescribed race plan of athletes making the first and last lap the fastest ran.

However, prior to the second run, athletes spent ninety minutes completing a prescribed task. The control group watched a nature documentary while the research group spent their time starting at a computer screen completing a cognitive task. When different letters of the alphabet were displayed, athletes had to respond by pressing various keys on the keyboard. The athletes then ran a second time trial following the same designated race plan.

Predictably, results clearly showed the cognitive fatigue group ran slower times than the control group. However, what caught the researcher's attention, was according to blood tests, heart rate results and ratings of perceived effort, the diagnostics were the same. In other words, despite running slower times in the second trial, the mechanics driving the body were the same.

The athletes just **felt** more fatigued.

In her paper titled *Cognitive fatigue and effects on physical performance during running*, published in the *Journal of Sport & Exercise Physiology*, Dr McMahon reported: "On a physiological level, participants invested the same resources, but these corresponded to worse performance". The athlete's performance directly correlated to what Exercise Physiologists call 'perception of effort.'

Feeling like we have to work hard directly impacts our ability to deliver results. This can serve us well when we have multiple projects, priorities, deadlines and demands. Knowing we have a finite amount of energy available each day, we can choose to invest our discretionary effort in the work we want to do.

However, the research undertaken by Dr Clare McMahon also highlights when we experience cognitive fatigue our capacity to deliver results can be severely restricted. This becomes most relevant when we start to consider our modern day existence and how our cognitive capacities are under constant demand.

Here are ten common activities that contribute to cognitive fatigue:

1. Managing multiple priorities
2. A lack of quality personal time
3. Trying to impress other people
4. Implementing a new behaviour
5. Managing regular interruptions
6. Restraining frustration or anger
7. Attending unnecessary meetings
8. Doing something you don't enjoy
9. Not seeing the value in your work
10. Coping with fear, worry or anxiety

Without adequate attention we forget our energy is a finite resource that needs to be managed. Failing to structure how we do our most valuable work means we burn vital effort on low value activities that don't contribute to higher levels of performance. This causes cognitive fatigue where we have inadequate energy for the moments that matter, for the defining moments when we need to resist the pull of preventative tension to keep moving forward.

When preventative tension is trying to derail our progress, we don't have adequate energy levels to do the work required. Instead of doing the work that delivers our desired future, we default to what makes us feel safe, comfortable, capable and successful. The work we prefer to do, know how to do, and is often easier for us to do, but this is rarely the work that builds a better future.

This sophisticated form of procrastination causes problems. We mistake a *sense* of progress with actually *doing* the difficult work that ultimately *delivers* progress.

The effect of cognitive fatigue is precisely what researchers Jonathan Levav and Liora Avnaim-Pesso were looking to explore when investigating the grueling schedule of judges in the Israeli parole system. Specifically:

Does the demanding schedule associated with the parole hearing process impact the judge's decision-making?

To manage the demand of the parole system, judges hear between fourteen to thirty-five cases a day, with an average deliberation time of six minutes. During this time they take two breaks. One in the morning and one in the afternoon. The rest of the day is spent listening, deliberating and deciding upon cases.

The researchers analysed over one thousand cases assigned to eight judges over a ten-month period highlighting a clear pattern. The possibility for a prisoner to receive parole was significantly higher in the morning or after each scheduled break, around 65%, before plummeting to near zero by the end of the day.

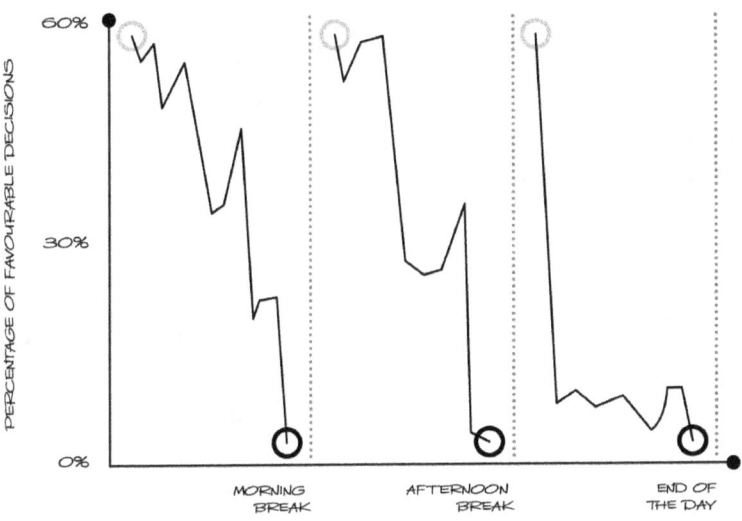

Figure 9: The impact of cognitive fatigue on Judges decision making.

This research reflects that, even for judges, effort isn't effortless. Their cognitive capability can take only so much listening, determining and decision-making before cognitive fatigue turns into default decision-making – which isn't overly positive news for parolees as the default decision for most judges is negative. Despite the presiding evidence, when judges are tired, cognitive fatigue presides and default decision-making means most prisoners stay behind bars.

This is true for any results based work requiring a period of sustained effort. Raising a child. Running a business. Making partner. Pitching a project. Changing your career. Finding a fitter you. Creating an inclusive culture. Balancing a busy life. Growing a relationship. Winning the Premiership. Rehabilitating a prisoner. Getting home on time. Caring for the elderly. Smashing the sales record.

All these jobs require sustained periods of effort. If our energy is not adequately managed, willpower can quickly turn into won't power and we stop doing the work that gets the job done. Having expended our energy and effort, we default to procrastinating rather than progressing. Doing rather than delegating; waiting rather than acting; complaining rather than contributing; and doubting rather than delivering. And then we wonder why success eludes us and seems so damn hard...

Which brings us back to the rubber bands. In the earlier example, our starting point involved two rubber bands of equal length. However, if we can delay the onset of preventative tension, metaphorically lengthening the rubber band, something significant happens. Just like a toned athlete who is flexible can stretch further, someone experiencing less tension can work for longer.

The reality is we don't always have the motivation to do the tasks that matter. By taming the tension involved in doing the work that drives results, we are able to work harder, for longer. This means we do more of the work that matters, and make more meaningful progress, while feeling less fatigued. Reducing the pull of preventative tension means our energy is invested for maximum impact.

Taming the tension means we can go further faster with *less* effort.

TAME THE TENSION

Any doctor with a degree of professional ethics will ask you a series of questions to start your consultation. She wants to find out what is going on to treat the fundamental issue rather than the symptoms you may initially be presenting. Writing a prescription without conducting a diagnosis would be malpractice.

SUCCESS HAS STRUCTURE

Yet every day we make the mistake of performance malpractice. We restrict our ability to get things done because we tend to ignore the situational or structural forces that shape people's behaviour. In a famous article, Stanford psychologist Lee Ross reviewed dozens of studies in psychology and noted that people had a tendency to attribute people's behaviour to *the way they are* rather than *the situation they are in*. He calls this tendency the Fundamental Attribution Error.

Consider this scenario. You are driving in traffic when someone races past you on the inside lane, only to cut back into traffic a few cars ahead of you. What we instinctively think is: that driver is reckless, selfish, irresponsible or dangerous. What we rarely consider is: why are they in such a hurry? We don't want to defend their actions because we don't want to excuse poor behaviour.

Yet this is part of the problem with the Fundamental Attribution Error. While we are quick to blame someone else's poor behaviour, we make justifications when we are in the wrong. Think of the last time you were driving erratically, made a wrong turn or didn't see a cyclist, someone else may have been cursing you. Were you making the same judgments about your own driving?

Performance quickly stagnates when we get stuck jumping to conclusions and judging people. For example when someone is driving erratically because they are running twenty minutes late to a crucial appointment, we may automatically label them a terrible driver. In our frustration, we fail to see the situation that they are in is causing them tension that is manifesting in the behaviour that we observe.

Of course, this doesn't mean we have to accept the behaviour. It just means we have to avoid the Fundamental Attribution Error if we want to source solutions that advance performance. This means portioning less blame on behaviours that we are observing and more focus on taming the tension causing the behaviour.

In 1977, the Commercial Banking Company in Australia started to provide all cheque account customers with access to Automatic Teller Machines (ATMs). A service that enabled customers to withdraw money outside of normal business hours. The original card the bank provided enabled customers to withdraw $25.

Initially, the debit card was retained by the machine and sent back to the customer once the funds had been debited from the account. However, with advances in technology, cards were soon being issued that debited the account directly and returned to the customer within the one transaction. This started creating a problem for the bank because, unfamiliar with the new process customers were taking their cash but leaving their cards in the machine.

Banks soon realised the cost of returning forgotten cards was outweighing the benefit of providing the service. So the decision makers got together to try and solve the problem. The result was making a small change to how the transaction took place that remains in operation today. Before machines dispense any cash, customers must first take their card.

Structuring your success is all about manipulating the two types of tension to make performance behaviours easier and preventative behaviours harder. Manipulating tension to drive desired behaviours is something you can see every day when you start to pay attention:

- Pay Pass makes spending money easy
- Amazon 1-Click lets you purchase instantly
- Opening a bank account is easier than closing one
- Drink drivers have to use an ignition lock to start their car
- Dieting companies control portion size to promote weight loss

The opportunities to tame tension and drive performance improvement are endless. Sadly, the all too common practice to advance performance is to revert to the tired and traditional method of punishments and rewards. An approach science has proven decreases the probability for improving performance. The alternative, and more influential factor for advancement, is to change our attachment. Taking the brave step to positively influence behaviour, by taming the tension preventing performance.

9 WAYS TO TAME TENSION

These nine methods to tackle tension come with a small caveat. They are not bullet proof. Working with clients over the past ten years to tame tension within a variety of contexts has taught me one thing. They rarely work in isolation. It is usually a combination of different methods that make the most impact.

So while there are different approaches to tackling the tension, the one thing I know from helping the best get better, is they consistently do these nine things. They continually scan their environment, observe the various tension points occurring and use these nine methods to consistently move things forward.

1. **CONTROL**
   Share the load

   Managers tend to hang onto things to feel in control. Leaders don't. One person being responsible for results will fail in a world of constant demand. There is just too much to do. Valuable work can only get done when people are encouraged and empowered to help deliver the meaningful work that makes results happen.

   Marco Pierre White is well known for operating a great restaurant. He cares about the quality of the food he delivers, but doesn't work on the bench. Instead, he trains and empowers Sous chefs to cook while dedicating his time to watch over the most important part of the entire operation. The kitchen.

2. **CONSTRAINTS**
   Work with adversity

   The movie character Jason Bourne can get out of most perilous situations. Just give him a rolled up magazine, a toaster and two minutes of idle time. Prisoners are similar. Have you seen the weapons they make using soap, a spoon and their toothbrush? They make do with what they've got and get the job done.

   I am not endorsing you go out and shank someone. Just accept you will rarely feel like you have the right amount of time, money, support or skills. This is what makes the difficult work valuable.

It's hard. Constraints are opportunity in disguise. You can either lose your way or find a way. It's up to you.

3. CAPACITY
Start saying no

Our natural desire is to feel respected and valued as someone who can get things done. So when we start to deliver we can get bombarded by requests, invitations and others' expectations. Feeling stretched once in a while is usually the consequence of being capable. Doing it all the time creates burnout.

The emotional exhaustion that comes from being overcommitted is caused by running yourself ragged to please everyone else. Saying yes to work without understanding what is required, or what time you actually have available. High performers learn to say no, saving their yes for their most important work.

4. FAILURE
Flip the fear

When you are living on the edge there is no room for failure. A doctor operating in emergency, a firefighter at the front line or a base jumper about to leap off the cliff. For these people, failure is not a luxury they can afford. For the rest of us there is a cushion. Fear is often our negative prediction of a false future.

The nature of risk is – things won't always work out. Expecting perfection, or criticising actions rather than redirecting effort, reinforces wrongness and discourages risk. You gain ground by learning from effort. You can't advance your career, your cause or your capability if you have to be right all the time.

5. FRUSTRATION
Fix what's broken

Most people are motivated to do good work until something, or someone, gets in their way. When progress is slow the easiest option is to allocate blame. The harder, but far more helpful approach, is to find out what's creating the issue, and seek a sustainable solution that reduces or removes the issue altogether. Issues such as: poorly designed systems, unnecessary steps slowing you down, policies that no longer reflect reality or limitations we are learning to accept. Being mindful of what regularly hinders your success will go a long way to helping you advance.

6. FATIGUE
Craft critical moves

When we have too many choices to consider we suffer from decision fatigue. Weighing up options about what to do wears us down because uncertainty, and the possibility of being wrong, makes us anxious. We default to avoiding a decision, or deciding to stick with the status quo, in order to stay safe.

Crafting the critical moves helps people focus their attention and limit decision fatigue. This is precisely why good restaurants spend time designing their menu. They know four pages of quality are much easier to digest than ten pages of quantity. Reducing choice actually assists customers make a dining decision.

7. ENGAGEMENT
Shrink the effort

We love to feel a sense of progress. If all we see is a whole lot of hard work, with no end in sight or success along the way, we become demotivated and stop doing the work that drives our results. Breaking tasks into smaller manageable steps enables small wins to be experienced and motivation to be maintained.

Traditional martial arts used to have two belt grades. White for beginners and black for advanced. The US Marines introduced the coloured belt system. Years of hard work got broken down into specific skills and incremental steps resulting in people achieving their black belt grading in a fraction of the time.

8. ENVIRONMENT
Structure your success

Our behaviours are deeply ingrained and so often hard to change. All too often we get frustrated when we try to change behaviour, whether that is our own or someone else's. Savvy influencers and change agents know that behaviour follows structure. So they build structures that drive desired behaviours:

- Childproof caps on bottles to prevent access by young hands

- Machines that don't operate unless a safety mechanism is secured

- Picture outlines on plates for dieters to manage portion sizes

9. ENJOYMENT
Make work fun

Making work fun is a great way to leverage your inherent motivation to do mundane, or meaningful work. This doesn't mean moving from serious to silliness, but adding a *gamification* element to enhance your engagement in the work you are doing. Create levels, keep score, track wins or build competition.

Air New Zealand decided to suspend the typically serious approach to safety by replacing the dull video with a more engaging and entertaining version. The new approach maintains the focus on safety but has more people paying attention. Not just in the cabin, but globally. The video series has gone viral. Smart.

In this fast paced, results orientated world, solving problems makes us feel productive. The pressure on achievement means we see tension as a problem rather than a positive sign we are doing valuable work. When we see a problem our natural tendency is to source a solution. But here's the thing. When we focus on the problems at hand, we fail to structure the success we want because we are too busy trying to prevent the things we don't want.

To make matters worse, even when we are dedicated and do the work to find a solution, we don't move any closer to achieving our desired future. We have just stopped something we don't want happening, from happening. The conditions, actions or clarity we require to advance our success, often remain unaddressed. This leads to the inevitable frustration and fatigue of inconsistent performance.

An important part of accelerating performance is being able to see the current reality. There may be existing problems that require attention, but problem solving on its own is an inadequate approach for advancement. Relying on the false belief that solving problems secures success, creates three side effects:

1. We get stuck solving problems. Sounds pretty obvious but can often be the very issue dragging us down and derailing our effort. We get so busy solving *situations* we fail to see the repeating *patterns* in our work, or personal life, creating the issue in the first place. We get stuck because the capability we build is problem focused not performance orientated.

2. We lose resilience for results. Spending time solving problems can easily become a full-time job. Whether we do it to demonstrate our value, help others or to stop sub-standard work, we get dragged into the detail that keeps us time poor and task fatigued. Working hard, but feeling like we are not progressing, causes us to lose focus, and resilience, for results.

3. We ignore motivation and momentum. Research in Neuroscience has shown people are most motivated when engaged in challenging work. When tension is seen as a problem to be solved, not performance to be delivered, we fail to access the most powerful lever for performance. Putting our skills to work in doing what motivates us, and matters to us.

STRUCTURE A SOLUTION

Having the presence of mind to positively impact tension is difficult. Tension can often be covert and complicated. And just like the tension itself, there are two tendencies we have for resolution. We can focus on the problem or structure a solution. One will keep you stuck. One will set you free. Here's a quick question for you:

Throughout your day, what's the ratio of time you spend between solving problems and structuring success?

Early in my consulting career I was fortunate to have the opportunity to work with one of Australia's premier circus troupes. During the early stages of my conversations with the circus, it became clearly evident that working with a consultant, much like their performances, was novel and unique.

Having been accepted to do the work, the owners were keen to give me an insight into the inner workings of the organisation and meet some of the stakeholders. Little did I know at the time, this experience was a little more hands-on than I anticipated or have experienced since.

On the first day, following a brief meeting with the senior leadership team, I was whisked away, and before you could say "welcome to the big top", was given a male leotard and told to change. Five minutes later I found myself in the middle of the big top, surrounded by circus staff and staring up at the big trapeze.

There were two other people dressed like me. One stepped forward, looked up at the trapeze bar dangling about twelve meters above our head and said: "I am standing directly underneath the trapeze bar. I'd like you to look up and stand directly underneath the platform above your head." It was at this point that I started to mildly panic thinking they were going to ask me to perform.

Aligned to the platform above my head, we were now standing approximately a meter and a half apart. Reaching out his hands and gesturing for me to do the same, our hands could nearly touch when they were both outstretched. Despite being aware of the point he was making, we weren't that far apart, my mild panic was starting to acclimatise to reality. We were really going to do this.

The next half an hour was a blur of instructions, trapeze technique, six-point safety briefing, and being introduced to the spotter controlling my harness. Ironically, Jules was the circus strong man. With everything in place, I climbed up the ladder and found my way, ungraciously, onto the tiny platform. High above the ground, the small trapeze no longer felt like I could almost touch it.

It now appeared like a large leap away.

On the ground, where the risks were low because my future reality wasn't reflected, the action seemed do-able, almost simple. However, twelve meters above the ground, on a tiny platform, with my knees knocking and everyone in the tent watching intently, the task felt far more difficult and demanding.

My mind worried about not making it, worried about Jules knowing what he was doing, doubting whether the harness would hold, and questioning whether consulting was *really* what I wanted to be doing as a career. It took me five minutes to calm my thoughts, find my focus and eventually make the leap.

Lowered to the ground a momentary hero I joked about canning consulting and joining the circus. Jules advised me, "Don't give up your day job," and shared that the exercise did have a point. The circus was in decline. People were protecting their tradition. Unprepared to make the leap to deliver a more modern day circus experience that people would pay money to attend.

As it turned out, the leap I made that day provided the catalyst for engaging the stakeholders of the circus in a conversation about change. On a personal level, the experience stuck with me as a significant life lesson about achievement.

You have to focus on the catch.

In any situation where there are risks and rewards we have a choice about where to invest our attention. When we focus on what we want or are trying to achieve, we naturally invest our skills and capabilities to make that happen. Equally, if we focus on what could go wrong, might not work or what needs to change, we attract our fears, doubts and false beliefs that drain our effort.

Definable Moments

When we switch from problem solving the current reality, to solution generating our future state, we experience a significant shift. We move tension forward. Reinforcing even the smallest amount of progress encourages a more positive focus that can be used to energise people into action. This is precisely why some forward thinking psychotherapists are using Appreciative Inquiry (AI) with patients.

Traditional psychotherapy involves an arduous archeological exploration into a client's past. They want to know about the past to be able to diagnose the issue and create some solutions for moving forward. In contrast, solution focused therapists who use AI don't care about archeology. They serve solutions.

Appreciative Inquiry practitioners use a common set of tools and techniques, founded on a serious of models, to access alternative solutions. Just like elite athletes watch footage to reinforce their ability to perform, AI therapists focus on encouraging clients to see solutions they are capable of achieving.

Conversations that deal directly with the problem occurring however, direct patients to generate possibilities for resolution. In their book *Switch*, Chip and Dan Heath provide a brief example from Brian Cade, a solution focused therapist based in Sydney, working with a couple as part of their marital therapy:

CADE: What would help make that happen for you?

WIFE: Well, there would be more understanding between us. We'd listen more to what each other are saying.

HUSBAND: Yes. At the moment, we really don't listen to each other. We just can't wait to get our own point across.

CADE: How could you tell the other person was really listening?

WIFE: In the face, I think. We'd perhaps make more eye contact. We'd nod in the right places.

HUSBAND: Yes. We'd both respond to what the other was saying rather than just attacking or ignoring it.

There are multiple benefits in making the choice to change focus from problems to solutions. One of the most significant is being able to leverage the difference between the size of the problem, and the size of the solution.

Big problems deceive us because we waste our time trying to find a silver bullet solution. We invest a lot of time, effort and resources trying to find the quick fix, easy solution or five steps people need to follow. We fail to recognise a series of small changes can have a significant impact. Just like a boat that makes a minor course change will, over time, arrive at a completely different destination.

This is why Brian Cade solves a communication problem, not a marital problem. Saving your marriage feels heavy and appears like a lot of hard work. Listening more intently to each other is much easier to do so gives the couple a sense of progress. Progress that helps the couple manage their marital issue through a series of steps. He is helping them learn how to structure their future success.

This methodology is not an uncommon practice. Marcus Buckingham wrote an International Bestseller called *Now, Discover Your Strengths*, to encourage people to find their strengths and learn how to use them for personal and career success. It is now widely accepted that one of the keystones to high achievement and personal happiness is being able to exercise our strengths.

The future is a function of where we put our attention. We have the ability to design, decide and deliver a better future. But equally, we can stagnate in our pursuit of success by focusing on the fear, doubt or false reality we imagine by falling victim to the Fundamental Attribution Error. Shifting from problem solving to a performance orientation is a critical step to securing success.

GO STRETCH YOURSELF

When trying to advance the pull of preventative tension is strong. The presence of this tension is positive because it lets you know you are doing the right work. Work that often stretches your existing capability, capacity and courage, testing your resolve to achieve the results you desire. Making the commitment to put your skills to work in that moment is the work that builds your better future.

Walk into any gym today and you will find resistance bands. Elastic bands or tubing that create resistance to movement, just like lifting a weight. Unlike weights however, instead of working against the force of gravity, resistance bands work against the tension applied to the stretched elastic material.

As the resistance band is stretched it becomes more difficult to move. The harder the tension, the more you have to work, and the greater gains you achieve to strength and muscle conditioning. The bands come with varying elasticity so people can find the right resistance for their workout.

Building your capacity for success is the same.

The tension you experience is just like that resistance band in the gym. You start by choosing the right level of resistance. Something that makes you work hard, but doesn't stretch you so much you can't work out again tomorrow. You seek out the right level of tension and then start to do the work.

When you feel the pull of resistance, you respond.

Each time you find a way to move the tension forward you are building your muscle memory for success. The more you work, the stronger you become and the more resistance you can handle. Tension is no longer avoided but accepted. You start to perform when other people panic. You find your strength rather than succumb to doubt. You find a way rather than fall in a heap. You define the moments that matter. You learn to succeed.

Go. Stretch yourself.

4
No Middle Ground

Success has no middle ground. When the defining moment comes, either you define the moment, or it will define you. Choose well and we move forward, choose poorly and we drop back and often face even harder choices. Don't choose at all and you passively accept whatever comes your way.

Making good choices is critical to making results happen.

When we make the choice to get the job done we must also accept the stretch associated with improvement. The results we seek only get realised when we pursue what we care about and commit ourselves to the moments that matter. Especially in the difficult moments that so often define performance.

AUSTRALIA'S FASTEST WOMAN

One morning late in 2013 Melissa Breen woke to learn that Athletics Australia had decided to cut her funding. The peak body for athletics in Australia deemed it was unlikely Breen would contest an Olympic or World Championship Final, so decided to direct their dollars into athletes they believed were more suitable.

Melissa Breen made a choice.

Despite the natural frustration and feeling disillusioned at the decision, she overcame her emotions and made the choice to focus on the future she desired. She didn't complain about why she should have got the money or that she had beaten others who secured some funding. She didn't lose control or espouse previous race results that proved she could run suitable qualifying times.

Definable Moments

She went back to work and became Australia's fastest woman.

At the State Championships in Canberra in 2014, Breen ran a time of 11.11 for the 100m, breaking the long-standing record of 11.12, set in 1994 by Melinda Gainsford Taylor. And she didn't stop there. Breen demonstrated her tenacity and elite ability later that day, by beating Olympic Gold medalist Sally Pearson. She sent back a clear message to Athletics Australia that things *were* working.

Learning about losing her funding, Melissa Breen didn't go on a tirade seeking blame, criticising her coach or questioning the selection committee. She went back to training. She put her skills to work and directed her energy, attention and effort, forward. A critical asset you must acquire if you want to advance.

Just like Melissa Breen, when we turn up and do the work that matters to us and motivates us, we get to make a choice. We can choose to serve position or performance **and** we choose to be passive *or* passionate. The decision we make about which we choose, determines our performance profile.

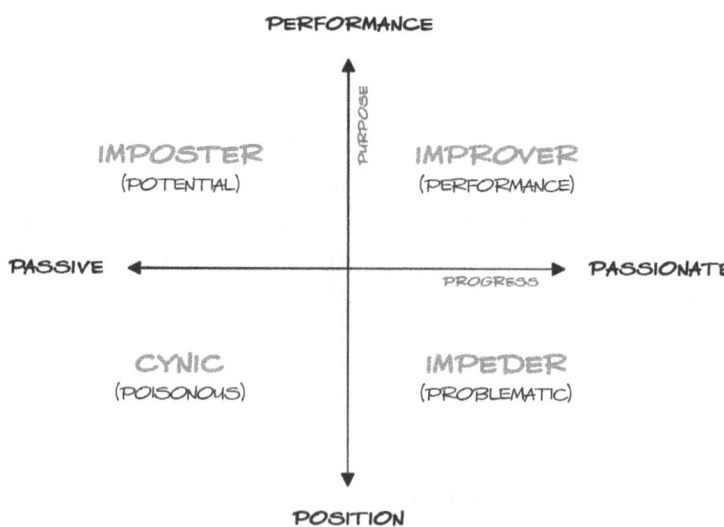

Figure 11: Purpose and progress determines our performance profile.

Purpose and progress are the two biggest drivers to performance. When we are going about our work, we are continually assessing our environment and making decisions based on how we are experiencing these two elements. We lose our way and get derailed by the difficult moments because of two main reasons:

1. We lose sight of our purpose
2. We stop making progress

Purpose and progress operate on a continuum. **Performance** relates to doing our highest form of work. Work we want to be doing. Work that is ambitious and challenges our skills and upsets the status quo. We inspire others and create a culture of inclusion. We have a positive impact and advance performance.

On the other end of the continuum is **position**. Where we **feel** like we are doing something significant, but are blind to the fact we are more concerned about who is right than what is right. Here, work feels hard, people often follow rules, results are leader reliant and controlling behaviour creates a lot of conflict.

The other axis contains the two dimensions of progress. Feeling that the effort we are investing is contributing to the results we are achieving.

When progress is slow, we get tired, frustrated or fed up, so stop putting our skills to work. We become **passive**. Our effort is protected rather than invested. **Passionate** people are the opposite. Committed to performance, they turn up, tune in to what needs to be done, and choose to put their skills to work to make a positive impact. This maintains progress and builds incredible momentum.

Every result you achieve, or roadblock you experience, is a consequence of your relationship to purpose and progress. Your level of success is determined by the decisions you make, the actions you take and the outcomes you serve.

PROFILING HIGH PERFORMANCE

People who deliver high performance are acutely aware of their location along the two continuums. While we predominantly operate within established personalities, preferences and patterns of behaviour, our performance profile continually changes during the day. Just like a compass rotates by degrees as we move, our performance profile also changes as we move up and down, or back and forth, each axis.

The critical skill to becoming a consistent Improver is discernment. Being savvy enough to see where you are, and skilled enough to make a shift to a more productive approach. When results seem elusive, rather than react, you can recalibrate your focus to ensure actions align with achievement. This starts with developing a reasonable understanding of the four performance profiles.

CYNIC
Passive and positional

Cynics are people who have given up but haven't shut up. This happens when we live in fear of anything that moves us beyond our comfort zone or current worldview. Cynics like comfort more than capability so will ignore different opinions and possibilities restricting performance. We typically justify this limitation by proffering our personal experience, position or preference.

Cynics desire a different future and want the world to change without making any personal change. The car manufacturing industry in Australia would best define this quadrant. For years, advances in automation and cost efficiencies have been threatening the industry. Despite needing Government subsidies to continue their operations, they failed to diversify. They failed to innovate. They failed to skill up workers for a future career. Cynicism killed the industry.

IMPOSTER
Purposeful but passive

Soon after a serial killer is caught, newsrooms will invariably interview all of the neighbours trying to find out what he was like. The answer is often the same. The perpetrator was quiet, unassuming, and didn't seem capable of doing such a thing. Imposters are similar. They are the unassuming serial killers of success.

This occurs when, on the surface, we appear to be doing a good job, but under scrutiny, we are really avoiding personal responsibility for our results. Imposter syndrome also occurs when we worry about whether we are good enough. Imposters are passive so tend to follow people or rules to remain safe from any risk, change or personal responsibility.

Imposters go to pointless meetings that have no purpose. They deliver the rah-rah but rarely the results. They protect the hierarchy rather than pursue their own ideas. They prefer to be passive so fail to progress. We become an Imposter when we stop investing our skills in things that we think matter.

IMPEDER
Passionate but positional
Impeders are passionately attached to their own position. In this mode, we work from a context of right and wrong often failing to consider alternate possibilities. While we often believe we are serving a higher purpose, we fail to see the only position we are endorsing is our own. Impeders spend the majority of their time 'right fighting' to reinforce their control, position or power. Impeders have a serious lack of discernment but a huge reserve of energy to fight for their worldview.

Quick to advocate their own position, Impeders make the world smaller, meaner and more difficult. Many taxi drivers in Australia are in this category. For years, they were the only real alternative to public transport and so ignored complaints of poor drivers, unclean cabs and unreliable service. When Uber arrived with immediate impact, rather than see that they needed to improve their service, they rallied, complained and tried to stop Uber from operating.

IMPROVER
Passionate and purposeful
The last quadrant is the Improver. Here, we are adept at seeing the world with discernment and can impact people, events and progress to drive performance. Focused on success, we understand the problem

is there to be fixed, the difficult person needs to be engaged and the set back is the platform for the comeback. This is precisely why we do the hard work that delivers advanced performance.

Improvers know followers are just as important as leaders and the right effort, given at the right time will deliver the right result. This is why we reserve our effort for the things that matter and learn to worry less about everything else. Performance doesn't reflect self-worth so rarely becomes personal. This opens the door to people and possibilities. Consequently, less time is spent moaning and more time is invested in actions that secure exceptional outcomes.

Bob Metcalf invented the Ethernet – the cable that allows computers to connect and communicate with each other. His system works on the principle that the value of anything increases when you have more in a network. For example, mobile phones weren't that effective when only the top twenty-five business people owned them. Product development and accessible pricing has now made the mobile phone an indispensable device. More phones create more value.

The more Improvers you have turning up to work the greater their value. They connect with others, have a high degree of influence and create a culture that people want to join, because people assimilate into the dominant culture. High performing cultures create exceptional competitive advantages.

Here's another way to consider the two axis on the performance model. The vertical asks: *What really matters?* The horizontal questions: *Do you care?*

LIABILITY AND LEVERAGE

When you contemplate these two questions against your current experience, the answers can be confronting. Look closely and you will see the performance liability you are carrying. The moments of misalignment between what matters to you and your willingness for action. These are the definable moments.

We improve performance and reduce our liability by taking action in these definable moments and accepting accountability for the results we are creating. This requires courage and a willingness to commit to doing the difficult work suspending the usual excuses we invent to abdicate ourselves from action. Psychologists refer to this as our 'locus of control'. The extent to which we are willing to accept we have control over what happens in our lives.

Internals have a strong belief that their actions control their outcomes. Their hard work and ability will lead them to achieve positive outcomes. Believing actions create consequences, internals also accept that things happen and the desired result is determined by whether they decide to take action. This action is derived from serving the desired outcome, not their prevailing emotions.

Externals have a tendency to believe external forces dictate their experience. People with an external locus of control believe things that happen in their lives are beyond their control. Even their own actions are the result of responding to external events such as explicit instructions, the influence of others, power, or complex issues that are too difficult to understand or impact.

The paradigm we prefer to operate from significantly impacts our performance integrity. Externals are influenced by their experiences and environment. So when things are working well, they are working well. When feeling challenged or stretched, their attitude and performance is impacted. In contrast, Internals rely on their capability to control performance. They do the work to drive the result, regardless of whether the conditions are conducive to achievement. The very definition of an Improver is the ability to deliver under duress or difficulty.

Comparing the difference between the two orientations, it becomes easy to see why an external locus makes it more difficult to achieve performance. Relocating the reasons to something external becomes inviting because we don't have to confront the current reality: that we don't have the time, energy, interest or capability to achieve the result we wanted.

Definable Moments

Externals prefer to stay within their comfort zone than accept the stretch for success. Developing the clarity to see when situations are not working takes courage.

Sadly, people with an external locus of control are just as likely to overlook the credit for their success, believing a mentor, great marketing or lucky moment, not their own dedication or drive, was the primary reason for personal success.

Internals on the other hand, will search inside themselves for insight, learning, and points of leverage to put into action when the next opportunity arises.

We rarely make the connection between our locus of control and level of success. How the choices we make regulate the results we achieve by either imposing constraints, or enabling our courage. Embracing the risks associated with achieving demonstrates an act of courage. Refusing to take risks, believing we are not able or responsible, reinforces our resignation.

Resignation reduces our locus of control diminishing one of the most powerful weapons we have for achievement. Choice. We make the shift from powerful to powerless. As Jim Collins reinforces in his book *Good To Great*, "…we are not imprisoned by our circumstances, our set backs, our history, our mistakes, or even staggering defeats along the way. We are freed by our choices."

In over ten years of business I have advised senior executives, sportspeople and serial entrepreneurs with a strong desire to accelerate their success. Everyone starts the same. Agreeing that responsibility for choices is a powerful paradigm shift that can lead to advanced performance. But many find it hard to make the decision in the definable moment: when the boss is breathing down their neck, the game is there to be won; the team is creating chaos, or the drycleaner who has pressed your favourite suit for the presentation tomorrow has just closed. These are the moments we can get derailed and either find a way or lose our way.

In today's results orientated world we have become ambitious but impatient. Strategies for success get packaged into sound bites diluting the difficult work that is always required to achieve results. Most motivational theories and daily doses of inspiration lose their impact when interacting with the real world.

Even if we do summon the courage to step up and improve our situation, we get frustrated when confronting the barriers associated with building a better future. Our emotional state gets hijacked because our plans and intentions are not having impact. We feel exposed so revert back to the external orientation where responsibility for progress is relocated to someone or something else.

Psychologist Daniel Goleman, author of the book *Emotional Intelligence*, wrote about the impact emotional hijacking has on our personal and professional lives. This change of state erodes resilience and impacts our ability to perform. When tensions accumulate over time, the most minor catalyst can erode our composure. If we succumb to this stress, we might lash out at someone, question our capabilities or lose energy and motivation to do what really matters. This can have untold consequences on the way we get things done. Results come, but often with some form of collateral damage.

Feeling in control is one of the strongest drivers to personal health and business performance. Recent research shows we are most motivated when engaging in meaningful activities that contribute to a positive sense of progress. There is a plethora of research supporting the benefit of control from the fields of positive psychology, motivational theory and neuroscience. But one stood out for me in particular as someone who advocates taking personal responsibility.

Psychologists Ellen J Langer and Judith Rodin conducted a study to evaluate the impact of personal responsibility on elderly patients at a nursing home. The study group was given encouragement and opportunities to make personal choices, such as tending to a small garden plant in their room. The control group was told the responsibility for good choices fell to the nursing home staff.

The outcome of the experiment showed when patients were given more control over their lives, not only did their happiness improve, but so did their levels of reported health problems. Despite a similar level of care, 71% of the control group reported more illness than their study group counterparts. Alternatively, the group encouraged to exert their personal control were more active, alert during activities and more socially engaged with staff and other residents.

Believing that our decisions matter and we control our future is a critical factor for consistent performance. Yet when we feel under pressure, stress increases and feeling like we are in control is the first thing to flee. To regain control we need to recognise choice. By refocusing our effort to the specific moments that contribute to meaningful progress, we reignite the knowledge, capability and confidence that once seemed so elusive. Here's how you can make a start:

1. **AWARENESS - Notice the tension**

    Take notice when you feel tension. Left unaddressed, it will compound and permeate your thinking, your feelings and your ability to function effectively. Research has shown that self-expression is the best antidote when we feel overworked and overwhelmed. So whether you confide in a colleague, draft the angry email or start a daily journal, expressing the stress, anxiety or annoyance you are feeling is a brilliant first step in taking back control.

2. **ALIGNMENT - Focus and forget**

    Worrying about things you can't control is a waste of time. So the next step is to separate the issues you can control from those you can't. This can easily be done on a piece of paper, in an Excel spreadsheet, or if resources are really limited, the dusty bonnet of a car, which I once did in rural Australia! The point is to separate the stresses where we have no control, and need to forget, with the issues where we can focus our effort and make a real impact.

3. **ADVANCEMENT - Small wins scale**

    Taking a multitude of problems and making them manageable improves our probability for success. Just like cutting through a piece of steel. Moving the welder randomly across the plate is far less effective than holding it stable in one spot. A focused approach is more powerful because it heats the metal quicker.

So too with the stresses we are trying to manage. Breaking the bigger issues into smaller tasks we can control, reduces the feeling of overwhelm and gives us greater confidence in our ability to achieve.

RESULTS NEED 'RESPONSE ABILITY'

Our ability to define the definable moments comes from feeling that we are free to make the choices that serve our desired outcomes. This freedom can only be found when we accept that we are responsible for creating the world in which we operate. In essence, this means what we experience is directly connected to the choices we have made in the past or are currently choosing to make.

When you reflect and realise your moments of liability, you will also see the moments you relocated your choice to someone or something else. Accepting our results are a function of our decisions, not our conditions, is as challenging as it is empowering. Moving beyond our conditioning or current circumstances and accepting we have the responsibility and initiative for choice. Even in the difficult situations or circumstances we find most challenging.

Victor Frankl was a psychiatrist who was imprisoned in the death camps of Nazi Germany. Frankl suffered extreme torture, the death of most of his family and lived through the most degrading circumstances imaginable. In his book *Man's Search For Meaning*, Frankl chronicles his experiences as an inmate in the concentration camp, and discovering the importance of finding meaning in all forms of existence, even the most brutal, which provide a reason for living.

During a particular moment of despair, alone and naked in a small room, he become aware of what he called "the last of the human freedoms". This was something his Nazi captors could not take away. While they could control his environment, how much he ate, what he did for work or how he was treated, Frankl observed one thing they could not take away. His identity. He could decide within himself how his circumstances were going to affect him.

> *"Between stimulus and response there is a space. In that space is our power to choose our response. In our response lies our room for growth and our freedom."*
>
> **Victor Frankl**

In this philosophy, Frankl provides a modern day challenge for all of us. Accept the 'response ability' we have in defining the most difficult moments of our life. The difficult moments which make us stronger and move us forward. Being response able doesn't mean being aggressive, manipulative, obnoxious or outspoken. It means recognising our responsibility to get the job done.

Easier said than done. Particularly when we avoid responsibility and relocate blame if the results don't go our way. It's the fault of our upbringing, the education system, our political leaders, the market conditions, our astrological chart, or the person we married. This approach distracts us from accepting that the decisions we are making, or failing to make, are creating the current reality that we are trying to change.

Even when we do come to terms with the concept of taking responsibility, there is still the realisation that the brain is a fundamentally flawed instrument when it comes to helping us navigate the decisions that direct our future.

HEURISTICS CAN BE UNHELPFUL

Daniel Kahneman is a psychologist and Nobel Prize Laureate for his work in advancing our understanding about how we make decisions. The prevailing belief prior to his research, with colleague Amos Tversky, was that humans are rational decision makers. We make decisions based upon logic and balancing the potential for profits and losses. What will we gain and what will we lose?

However, in their study of heuristics and the tools we use when making decisions, Kahneman and Tversky found that our decisions are anything but rational. In one of their well-known experiments, two strangers are brought into a room. One person is given ten $1 bills and told to divide the money between himself and the other person, any way he liked. Once this has been done, a "take it or leave it" ultimatum is offered to the recipient with one catch: if they decide not to take the money, both people walk away with nothing.

On the surface this is a fairly straightforward economic choice. Having arrived with nothing, any amount offered is a profit, so you accept the deal. Right? However researchers found people were actually more likely to reject the lower offers of $1 or $2. Recipients refused the lower offers out of spite, disappointment or principal. The rational decision was quickly overtaken by irrational emotion.

There have been a host of fascinating books that have explored the reasons why we have difficulty making effective choices. *Predictably Irrational* by Dan Ariely, *Decisive* by Chip and Dan Heath and *The Cost of Everything* by Eduardo Porter are books I would recommend for further reading. One common denominator to their collective content is the impact of cognitive bias. The rules and creative short cuts we take to make decisions when our mental real estate is crowded, and we feel overwhelmed and under pressure.

Cognitive biases can be hard to identify because they occur in our subconscious. *The Cognitive Bias Codex*, by John Manoogian and Buster Benson, offers a great starting point as it decodes many of the known biases that impact our decision-making abilities. Here are twelve biases worth paying particular attention to if you are working to achieve advanced levels of personal or professional performance:

1. **AMBIGUITY EFFECT - Seeking positive probabilities**

    This bias is where our decision-making can be affected by a lack of clarity. When uncertain, we have a tendency to choose options where a favourable outcome is known, over an option where a favourable outcome is unknown. This can result in endless information seeking, or defaulting to the routine decision, rather than taking a risk that may render a more valuable outcome.

2. AVAILABILITY HEURISTIC - Memories maneuverer reality

Our tendency to take a mental short cut in accessing immediately available memories, examples or experiences when evaluating a specific topic, concept or decision. For example, patients who experienced pain in the final fifteen minutes of their procedure, despite having little pain throughout the operation, will recall the experience as largely painful and uncomfortable.

3. CONFIRMATION BIAS - Reality confirms rightness

Our tendency to look for, interpret and focus on information in a way that confirms our existing beliefs. Too much of this and we get stuck making decisions using the old stories that no longer serve us. For example, when we were seven we may have thought capsicums tasted terrible, and so have avoided it completely ever since, despite knowing our palate has probably changed.

4. CONSERVATISM BIAS - Challenged to change

This bias refers to our tendency to believe prior evidence, and not amend our perspective, when new evidence or data is presented. This can occur in areas of personal judgment, scientific experiments, changing technology or world events where, despite prevailing evidence of change, we defend the status quo, current thinking or 'the way things are done around here'. A level of skepticism with evolution is prudent. Too much and performance suffers.

5. FRAMING BIAS - Context controls reality

Our tendency to make two different decisions when provided with the same information that is framed differently. Essentially as to whether we lose or gain something. Losing something is perceived as more significant than gain. This is why, when watching an infomercial in the middle of the night, you will hear messages about losing weight rather than getting in shape; reducing the stress of debt instead of building financial freedom; and eradicating facial wrinkles in place of coming to terms with growing old gracefully.

6. **HINDSIGHT BIAS - Past performance predicted**

    Our tendency, after an event has occurred, to see the event as having been predictable, despite having little or no objective basis for predicting it. Hindsight bias may cause memory distortion creating limitations for the essential learning or insight we require for advancement. For example, a leader uncertain about a course of action may seek out advice, reinforcing they knew it was the right decision all along, when things work out. This is why the hindsight bias is also referred to as the 'knew it all along' effect.

7. **HYPERBOLIC DISCOUNTING - Preferring immediate results**

    Our tendency to prefer rewards that occur sooner rather than later. The longer we wait the more we mentally 'discount' perceived value. Even if the probability of the delayed alternative will provide greater gains. This bias can be largely overcome by scaffolding success. Breaking down long-term larger rewards into more manageable tasks and reinforce progress regularly.

8. **ILLUSIONARY TRUTH EFFECT - Frequency makes factual**

    Our tendency to believe certain information is true because we have heard it frequently. Some common examples include: we only use 10% of our brain, swimming after eating is dangerous, and habits get formed in thirty days. We subconsciously attribute more truth to information we hear more frequently.

9. **INFORMATION BIAS - Information before action**

    This bias is when we believe that the more information we can acquire to make a decision, the better. Even if that additional information is irrelevant to the decision. This is a good bias to check when success has stalled. Often we want to read more, learn more or know more to avoid risk. Avoidance is also an action, just not a very effective one for furthering performance.

10. OMISSION BIAS - Inaction over action

This bias describes our tendency to doing nothing than doing something. We prefer inaction than taking an action that may turn out to be wrong. Leaders can find this bias particularly frustrating when delegating to staff who avoid making decisions. When people fear making the wrong decision, or being punished for a mistake, they choose safety by avoiding acting altogether.

11. OPTIMISM BIAS - Positivity as placebo

Our tendency to believe we are less at risk of experiencing a negative event compared to others. This is often seen in people who are overly positive, and lack real world discernment, leaving themselves vulnerable to the difficult events that do arise. This bias is worth paying attention to when working with people who mistake inspiration and motivation with ambition.

12. SOCIAL COMPARISON BIAS - Capability through comparison

Our tendency to have feelings of dislike and competitiveness with someone who we believe is physically, or mentally better than ourselves. This bias can sometimes serve a positive agenda as it highlights the characteristics or capabilities we aspire to have but feel we don't yet hold. When people are unaware, or the bias is left unaddressed at workshops, meetings, or within a team, people work hierarchically, not healthily, impacting performance.

These biases create a core difficulty with decision-making. What we perceive as clear and rational decisions can be plagued by cognitive bias. The subconscious traps that deviate our judgment creating unintended consequences that keep us stuck. Our biases cannot be completely eradicated, but they can be mitigated so we don't sabotage our ability to make successful decisions.

DELIBERATE DECISION MAKING

When a professional swimmer launches off the blocks at the start of a race you rarely see them surface and start thrashing about wildly. Despite the desire to go faster than their rival, the desire to touch the wall first, and the desire to win their event, they don't mistake moving their arms with getting somewhere.

They leverage their technique. They pay attention to their stroke rate; kicking efficiency, turn technique and breathing to power their body through the pool. Elite swimmers seem to be moving effortlessly because they have learned to leverage technique. It's less about effort and more about impact.

Making decisions that move us forward is the same.

Having a process that helps us make effective decisions when we are under pressure, need to perform, and most exposed to cognitive bias, is crucial. The decision making process we use must be agile, adaptable and effectively simple. Anything that proves to be too complicated or arduous opens the opportunity for cognitive bias to sabotage the decisions that serve our success.

Event x Choice = Outcome

This simple process supports decision making by restricting cognitive bias and embracing our 'response ability' to serve the outcome we want to achieve. Let's explore each component in a little more detail (and a slightly different order):

Event refers to the catalyst that threatens our motivation or momentum. The negative comment that was said, a colleague that gets promoted, an obstacle we have to overcome, or the self-doubt that plagues any successful person as they stretch for something more than they have now. We feel tension here.

Outcome reflects the desired result we are working to achieve. The aspiration or ambition we have chosen to invest time, money, effort and resources to achieve. Not because we have to but because we want to. It matters to us.

Choice recalibrates the event we experience with the outcome we desire. Our locus of control will determine the level of choice we will explore and execute. Choice provides the chance to leverage our skills or reinforce limitations that keep us stuck, stagnant and stationary. This is where we want to take action.

The process also forces us to interact with the two forces of failure when it comes to making and executing successful decisions. Overcoming the initial unhelpful **emotions** that may have been triggered by the event, and openly considering the range of **actions** that will best serve our desired outcome.

One of the fundamental differences between Improvers, and everyone else, is where they focus. Improvers are influenced by external events, but maintain a strong focus to the outcome they are trying to achieve. They embrace their 'response ability' and focus on sourcing solutions that serve their future. The nature of their energy is positive and performance orientated.

The other performance profiles have a predominantly external locus of control and get caught in the forces of failure. They lose perspective on their ability for choice, reinforcing the results they desire are out of their control. Under duress, they focus on external issues, often blaming, accusing or highlighting limitations of solutions, with little insight or acknowledgement to their own behaviour.

Event x ~~Choice~~ = Outcome

Our ability to get the job done improves significantly when we start to realise every outcome we experience is a result of the choices we make. Does your boss restrict your ideas *or* do you run everything past your boss for approval? Will more money help you start your business *or* are you scared to back yourself? Are you constantly busy or causing yourself stress because you can't say no?

Of course there are people, projects and problems that make it difficult. These difficult moments may impact you, but they don't have to define you. Making it through the hard part is the price we pay for peak performance. If difficulties were the defining factor for success nobody would ever achieve. But they do.

And that is the challenge. When you are experiencing success, make sure to pay attention to what is working, and keep doing that as much as possible. And just as importantly, when success is eluding you, pay attention to the decisions you are making, or failing to make, and adjust your choices accordingly. These five indicators will help you focus on consistently investing in your future success:

1. GET STARTED... AND FINISHED

Some of the work we want to get done is hard to start. Like blowing up one of those skinny balloons. You need the lungs of an elite marathon runner, and a long deep breath, to force enough oxygen for the balloon to inflate. Some other things are easier to start but much harder to finish. Like maintaining a diet or healthy exercise routine. Knowing which type of work you are doing allows you to invest your energy effectively right at the moment that matters most.

2. STOP DOING THINGS

Doing things is all about fulfilling a set of conditions you believe are necessary to get what you want. When we fail to identify the underlying issues causing our tension, we tend to solve symptoms not create solutions. I once coached a woman to not commence her PhD but instead start a conversation with her father whose approval she was ultimately seeking. Taking *specific steps* that move you directly toward your desired outcome accelerates success.

3. ACTION ISN'T PERFECTION

People who get the job done have a bias for action but realise actions are rarely accompanied by perfection. Responding to set backs is just part of success. So when one action doesn't succeed, they take a second, third or fourth action to get the job done. Barriers are not an end point but the next departure point for further action. This process of action and re-action forms the foundation for people with a mindset for advancing performance.

4. ACCEPT YOUR MEASURE

Once you make a conscious choice to stop pursuing something, you have found your measure. It may be the measure of your energy, your capability, your influence, or your level of interest at the time, but you decided to stop. There are times, of course, when this is entirely appropriate, but if the scenario reflects that your measure isn't measuring up, then step up. Get to work developing the skills, strategy or smarts that will keep you in the game and get the job done.

5. ACT OR FORGET

Complaining is the voice of helplessness. Often reserved for when we feel most stuck and cynical; when we fail to see that we want something to be different, but avoid the difficult decisions that can make it happen. Risking our reputation, shifting a long held paradigm, stepping into an uncertain future or having to admit we tried, but failed. In these situations we need to do the difficult work to achieve what we desire, or move on and redirect our energy, enthusiasm and commitment to something more gratifying. Moaning about what you can't change, or aren't prepared to change, will make you bitter and boring.

The bottom line is the choices you make, regardless of how small or slight, alters the trajectory of your experience. You make your choices, and then your choices make you. And this doesn't mean taking on the most difficult issue to have the most impact. Delivering the small wins can easily scale into significant success.

SMALL LEADS TO SIGNIFICANT

Starting small can be a hard concept to consider if you are feeling time poor and task fatigued. The desire to quickly reduce the stress we are feeling seduces us into seeking the fastest solution. So we embrace the quick fix or easiest option, which is often less successful or sustainable, reinforcing our sense of stress.

Clare is a friend of mine who is terrible with time. She constantly rushes from one thing to another and always arrives late usually offering her apologies before she even sits down. She is flustered trying to focus on six urgent things she needs to get done while we catch up to converse around the issues of the day. Her work is demanding. Her schedule is full. Her headspace is crowded.

Every year Clare crashes. Trying to please everyone all of the time leaves her exhausted. She declares life to be too demanding and decides to escape to a lifestyle retreat to detox from the pressures she places herself under. Clare doesn't want to face the reality of her choices and so substitutes any real chance to make change with spending time in the tranquil hills of New South Wales.

Inevitably, three weeks after returning home with valuable insights and a fresh perspective for more purposeful living, Clare is stressed again. This cycle has been occurring for the past three years with no signs of stopping. Clare would be much better served doing the work to create a life she didn't have to escape from every year. Managing the smaller issues she could scale into larger success.

The concept of small steps leading to significant success was first introduced to me over fifteen years ago when sitting down with a financial planner. Just starting to earn a substantial salary, I wanted to make my money work for me. Specifically, structure a savings plan in order to purchase my own property.

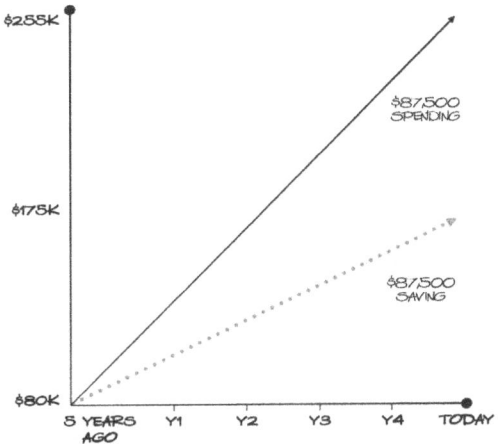

Figure 12: Saving every salary increase can result in significant savings

Definable Moments

Looking at the diagram he drew for me, Tim shared his two secrets to financial security. First, commit to saving at least half of every future salary increase you receive. This provides the lifestyle upgrade you deserve while increasing your wealth. Second, save small, save often and start now.

We fail to save because we wait for what we think is a suitable sum of money to save. The problem is we never get there because $500 is much harder to find than $50 because we live to our means. When our salary increases so does our lifestyle: the restaurants we frequent, the wine we drink and the goods we buy. Our spending increases proportionally to our salary.

Reflecting on this retrospectively, adopting his approach would have seen me save $87,500, easily accounting for the house deposit I wanted to save. Being unaware at the time about how small success can scale into significant results, meant my financial goals fell behind where I could have been.

Overlooking the small choices we have, and can execute easily, can be difficult when the world appears to be closing in and all consuming. We get busy being busy, reject our own reality and close down the simple choices that have the possibility to create meaningful change. Change that, despite being small, can scale over time and be the difference between status quo and success.

Defining the definable moments cannot be taught - but it can be learned. Making the decision to turn up and take the necessary actions that serve your desired outcomes. Starting with the small everyday events we experience in life. Events such as: running late, hearing disappointing news, missing your usual train home or having to work with a difficult deadline.

These everyday events provide the training ground to develop your capability to perform under pressure.

RESULTS REFLECT REALITY

The biggest barrier to securing future success is when people are unaware or unwilling to accept responsibility for the results they are creating. This lack of awareness, or preference to locate problems outside of themselves reinforces the belief they have no responsibility for their result. This restricts them further, increasing their frustration as progress and performance become more elusive.

How we perceive our problems, and where we choose to focus our energy, are the keys to advancing performance. The more you avoid your choice, the more you lose your voice, the more likely you are to be ignored, and the more you limit potential and possibility.

Joy works at the Baby Bunting near where I live. She is uninspired, unhelpful and unapproachable. If you do manage to attract her attention, her responses are short, her service is slapdash and she rarely raises a smile.

The funny thing is Joy spends the same amount of time at work as Lucy, but Lucy is engaging, caring and customer orientated. Joy has decided that work is a drain and she would rather be somewhere else. Lucy sees her platform to engage and empower new parents, so offers them much needed clarity every day.

Joy undoubtedly has her reasons for doing the bare minimum. Maybe she's tired, maybe she feels stuck, or maybe she is mistaking the common questions concerned new parents ask as mundane work. Sadly, Joy is missing the point. Just because she feels stuck doesn't mean she is stuck. She has a choice.

Right now you have a choice. You can accept your current reality and keep doing what you are doing, or you can choose to change. You can't do both. You can accept your limitations or start working on them. You can start saying no or say yes to every random request. You can protect yourself from hurt or learn to trust. You can hide from your work or do great work. The choice is yours.

I am merely advocating you accept your 'response ability' when deciding.

DEFINABLE MOMENTS

Making choices is a challenge because we have to start to come to terms with uncertainty. This always involves risk and risk reinforces our need for safety. But it is obvious from every success we see in the Boardroom, on the sporting field, with the latest start up, or the rock star about to launch their latest album. Those who secure their success rise to the occasion.

This chapter is a manifesto for making choice. Once this habit is ingrained you start to find your freedom. When you find your freedom, you start making choices and initiating actions that drive results. And this changes everything. You become the curator of your own experience. The more you choose, the more momentum you build and the more opportunities you generate.

You realise your gifts, redefine your work and raise the bar.

5
Build successful habits

The man in front of me is yelling at the teenage cashier because he has been waiting in line too long. While he rants and raves about customer service and taking his custom elsewhere, he is failing to see *he chose* to stand in line for as long as he did. Classic relocation. The only move I saw him make was to look around to see if another employee was running down the aisle to help serve.

As it turns out, the young cashier started two days ago, forgot the protocol of pressing the button under the counter that alerts other staff that she needs help, and so people were waiting a little longer than usual. As for the unhappy customer in front of me, it was easier for him to stand and fume rather than take responsibility to go and find someone else who could serve.

And that's the point.

When some kind of interference impedes our progress we default to taking the path of least resistance. Moving from stuck to sourcing a solution can take energy that we don't have or don't want to invest. So despite having the choice to move things forward, we default to the easier decision of defending the status quo, just like the man getting hostile about waiting five minutes longer in line. When we design habits for success we must remember our preference for the path of least resistance and so make any new habit easy to at upon.

CHOICE ARCHITECTURE

Anne Thorndike is a primary care physician at Massachusetts General Hospital in Boston. She is also a behavioral scientist who knows that new habits are hard to form. When she wanted to change the eating

Definable Moments

habits of people who used the hospital cafeteria, she knew she had to make choosing the right foods easy.

Thorndike and her colleagues believed that by changing how the food was displayed in the cafeteria, they could get people to eat healthier. Rather than having to focus on willpower or selling an inspirational message to motivate people into action, Thorndike changed the choice architecture. Essentially, 'changing the way food and drinks were displayed' in the cafeteria.

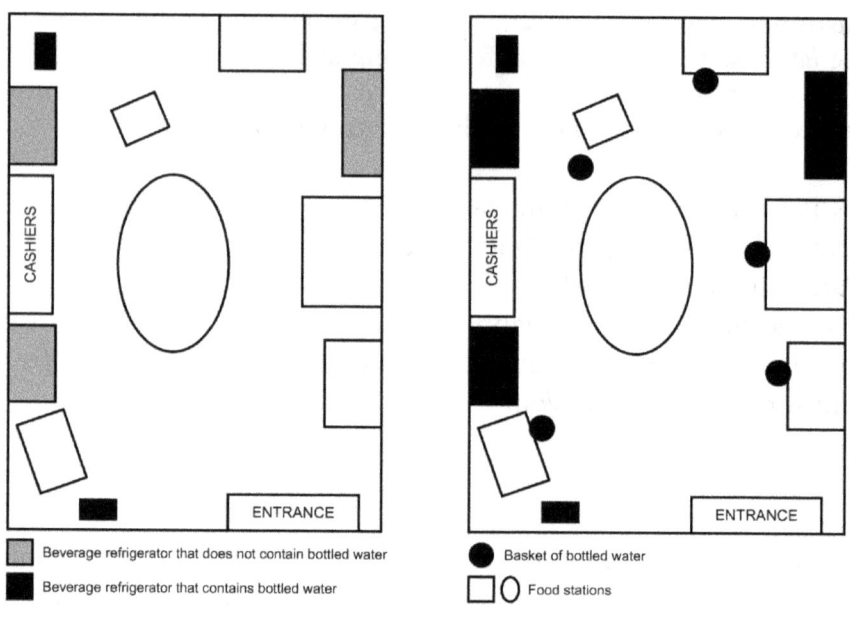

Figure 12: Changes made to the choice architecture to drink more water.

The researchers started by changing the choice architecture of the drinks in the cafeteria. Initially, there were three main refrigerators filled with cans of soft drink. Thorndike made sure water was added to each refrigeration unit and placed baskets of bottled water throughout the room.

Over the next three months, soft drink sales reduced by 11.4% while bottled water sales increased by 25.8%. There were no signs displayed, nobody promoting a particular choice or people being told about the study being done. Anne Thorndike just made choosing water an easier decision to make.

For years, retailers have used choice architecture to encourage consumers to purchase their product. In the best selling book *Nudge*, Richard Thaler and Cass Sunstein provide various examples of how our everyday decisions are shaped by the choice architecture we encounter. Supermarkets charge a premium for eye level product placement because this is where we purchase most of our goods. Retailers will rarely have cluttered clothing racks so people can feel the garment and get a 'sensory test run' increasing their probability to purchase.

The choice architecture we create in our approach to life, whether consciously or otherwise, can also influence our own productivity and performance:

- If you don't have a calendar management system and anyone can schedule your time, meeting more than working is probably your default.

- If you are constantly connected to your smartphone and rarely detoxing from digital demands, feeling constantly tired is probably your default.

- If you see the difficult moments as a chance to put your skills to work, then being able to overcome adversity or challenge is probably your default.

When we establish a choice architecture that makes difficult choices easier to execute, we increase our chances of making good choices under pressure. And this matters, because in the definable moments, we rarely rise to the occasion, we usually revert back to default decisions. In other words, when our energy is waning and our willpower is low, we tend to take the path of least resistance.

Peter Gollwitzer, a psychologist at New York University, has conducted some interesting research on how *preloading specific triggers* helps motivate people do what matters in the moments that matter.

The benefit of preloading resides in making a future commitment to take positive action. Making a decision in advance helps to mitigate the distractions that can derail our best intentions.

This is particularly evident when people have to manage difficult decisions. In one study, using 'action triggers' to achieve easy goals provided little variable benefit, with only a slight increase from 78% to 84%. However, when it came to the harder goals, action triggers almost tripled the chance of success, with successful achievement moving from 22% to 62%.

These results also translated into a study of patients recovering from hip and knee surgery. The patients encouraged to use action triggers, such as 'write down when and where you plan to walk today', recovered faster and gained post surgery joint function much faster than patients with no action triggers.

Gollwitzer believes that preloading an action trigger creates a habit response. The benefit of building habits is they happen automatically. We can take the appropriate action without expending too much energy. The more we reinforce the right behaviours, in the moments that matter, the more we develop a habit for high performance. Consistently choosing the behaviours that drive results, encourages progress and produces performance integrity.

We get the job done all of the time – not just some of the time.

PERFORMANCE INTEGRITY

Motivation is often confused with inspiration, but in reality, they are two very different concepts. Inspiration often describes the catalyst moment where we find a spark. It may be in the shower, at a conference, hearing someone speak or watching something on television that moves us emotionally. Inspiration is the feeling we have that stimulates our thoughts to start, change or conquer something. But inspiration is perishable. It doesn't last forever.

BUILD SUCCESSFUL HABITS

Motivation on the other hand describes the deep internal drive we need to achieve a specific aspiration or ambition. The jobs included at the start of this book provide a snapshot to some of the aspirations we sometimes hold. This may include starting your own business, or trying to find a better balance to living life. Motivation is the fuel that drives our effort to build a better future.

BJ Fogg is the founder of the Persuasive Technology Lab at Stanford University. He spends his time studying, lecturing and speaking about: "creating persuasive systems that support behaviour change through ethical means." The core of his work is focused on understanding how habits form and function. In particular, how habitual behaviours that have impact, are activated and encouraged.

When we experience a preloaded trigger, the right levels of motivation and execution can make a profound difference to achievement. While motivation and execution work independently of each other, the premise to producing performance integrity is getting them to compliment each other. Much like Hayden and Langer, Gin and Tonic, Torvill and Dean or Jobs and Wozniak.

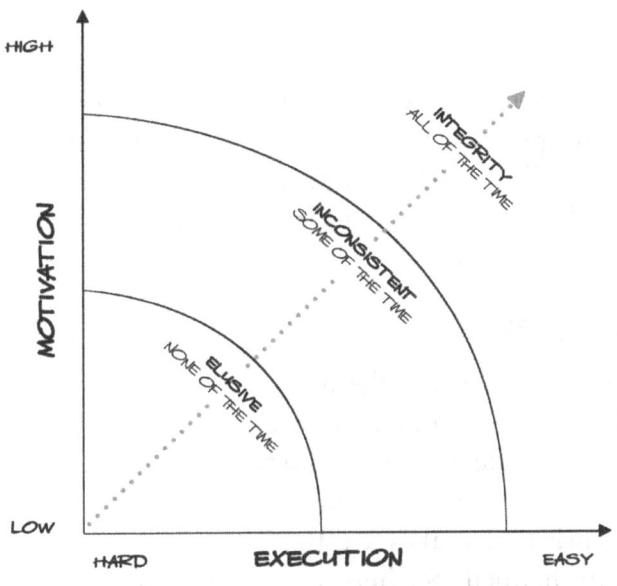

Figure 13: High motivation and easy execution creates performance integrity.

How consistently we perform under pressure is largely dependent on how well we integrate motivation and execution into the work that matters:

1. Results prove **elusive** when performance behaviours are unlikely to occur because motivation is low and the actions we need to take are too hard.

2. **Inconsistent** performance occurs when motivation levels fluctuate, or when the actions we need to take are too complex or difficult.

3. When our motivation is consistently high, and the result we want to achieve is compelling, clear and achievable, performance **integrity** is produced.

The two anomalies that arise in delivering results can also be seen in the above model. Being, when certain results *are* complex or difficult, but our motivation is high, we get the job done. And, when our motivation *is* low, but the result we want to achieve is easy to execute, we also get the job done. But, these options are far less sustainable than creating the structures that serve our success.

Performance integrity is created when we engage the right behaviours, at the right time, to achieve the right result. Success is secured more easily when we preload a trigger, possess high motivation, and make the work that will make the results happen much easier to do. For this to be achieved, three components need to be considered: motivation, execution and a trigger.

1. MOTIVATION

Most of the time we make the mistake of using external rewards to motivate desired behaviours. Rewards work for repetitive or simple tasks but are less effective in competitive or complex environments. All too often they actually detract from the inherent motivation of doing the work that makes a difference, moves things forward and makes results happen. So here are three alternative ways you can maximise the inherent motivation of work to be done:

A. **Challenge**
Staying stationary within a world of rapid change is a dangerous posture for anyone who desires success. Offering a positive challenge can be a terrific catalyst for progress, change and growth. High performance happens when we accept the tasks that move us beyond our existing capability. Fulfilling potential is deeply satisfying and ensures we continually advance our existing skills.

B. **Autonomy**
Nothing motivates people more than giving some clear direction and then getting out of the way. Giving people the space to operate and the opportunity to bring their energy, ideas and innovative thinking to what needs to be done. Disrupting complacency, delegating responsibility and allowing capability to flourish, offers people freedom and autonomy in how they engage in work.

C. **Purpose**
Autonomous people who stretch themselves perform well. But when we work in service of a greater purpose, we often achieve more. Motivation escalates quickly when the work we are undertaking is meaningful, is making a positive impact or aligns to our deepest values. Money matters, but the greatest uplift we can achieve to motivation is taking the time to make work meaningful.

2. EXECUTION

When motivation is high, but the task we are doing is difficult to accomplish, making the task easier to execute, stimulates success. The mistake many people make in trying to advance performance is investing in more skill development. Having the right skills to succeed is important, however when it comes to *high performance*, a lack of skills rarely proves to be the source of poor results.

We make much greater gains when we reduce the friction points preventing performance from being achieved. Success is further advanced when we focus on the definable moments when the desired behaviours need to be delivered. Here are three things worth remembering when you want to reduce friction:

Definable Moments

A. Risk

We are wired to fit in with the crowd because being part of a group leaves us less vulnerable than being on our own. It's evolutionary. People conform to the predominant culture. Expecting people to make a stand, or speak out against the status quo, involves risk. Even if the behaviour is easy to do, deviating against what feels socially acceptable complicates our ability to act. So making the desired behaviours acceptable to do is the starting point for any success.

B. Rules

Rules have a bad reputation because they have been predominantly used to restrict people. Poor policies that get created to prevent behaviours we don't want, like that time Bob from accounts wore his shorts into work one day. But removing ambiguity by creating rules around the behaviours we want to build becomes an effective tool for execution. When done well, rules help to focus our attention, empower positive action and facilitate a sense of progress.

C. Routines

Routines are the rituals we complete that connect our risk, effort and results. They are a set of established behaviours we implement to make the work easier to do. Stretching before running, digital detox days, stand up meetings or never ordering the same meal as a couple. Routines are the rituals we establish that reinforce behaviours that drive progress and deliver performance. Designed well, routines become a powerful ally in building high performance habits.

3. TRIGGER

Triggers refer to the prompts, cues or calls to action that provide a catalyst to engage in a particular action or behaviour. The sound in the airplane cabin just before an announcement is a trigger to make passengers listen. The calendar alert that sounds thirty minutes before your meeting is a trigger to get going. Your stomach growling mid-morning is a trigger to eat because you are hungry.

Triggers are important to understand because they are the starting point for producing the successful habits we want to engage. There are three common types of trigger that promote us to take positive action:

A. **Catalyst**

When we lack the desired motivation to do something catalyst triggers work well. A specific catalyst delivered at the right moment can activate our awareness that there is an action to take. For example, your morning alarm is a trigger to start your day. When it comes to catalytic triggers, the timing is more important than the type. A catalyst will only work when it gets delivered in the moment when the desired action needs to be taken.

B. **Commitment**

Commitment triggers encourage behaviour by reinforcing that the desired action is easy to do. One click conference registration, automatic insurance renewal, advertising mail and 'do you want fries with that?' are all examples of these kinds of triggers. For commitment triggers to work motivation needs to be high. The trigger merely makes us aware there is an action to take, and encourages our ability to execute by reinforcing the action is easy to perform.

C. **Confirmation**

When motivation is high, and the task is easy to execute, confirmation triggers signal to engage in the appropriate behaviour. Reaching for someone's hand when you meet is a signal to shake. Seeing the red light turn to green is a signal to enter the intersection. Hearing the crescendo at the end of the concert is a signal to show your appreciation. These triggers don't serve to motivate us or simplify the task. They merely reinforce or remind us what to do.

Building performance integrity becomes most important when preventative and performance tension intersect. This is when tension is hardest because both forces are fighting our subconscious for dominance. This is when we decide to move forward or drop back and why designing for our least resistance default is so important. When we motivate positive behaviours, and make them easy to execute, we start to build a habit for high performance.

We develop the habits that help us move forward faster with *less* effort.

HIGH PERFORMANCE HABITS

Success can often prove elusive because sustaining the desired behaviours that drive the results we desire is hard work. Even when people are motivated to perform at their peak, their ability to execute can be easily impeded, leaving the commitment for action largely unrealised. The initial feelings of inspiration get eroded over time and original promises turn into old patterns of behaviour.

If we have this incredibly complex brain, that is capable of growing, changing and adapting to our environment, why is consistent performance so hard?

A reasonable starting point to answer this question comes from research at Duke University and published by the *Association for Psychological Science*. Researchers found that over 40% of the actions people performed each day weren't due to decision-making, but habits. In a sense, this is positive as the habits we create protect our precious energy resources. Reducing the repetitive work we undertake saves our mental resources for the work that needs a higher level of consideration, collaboration or commitment.

On the other hand, habits decrease our neurological activity because they occur subconsciously, making them appear automatic. If 40% of our decisions are being made from habitual response rather than conscious choice this means our decisions flow from automated behaviour using the stimulus response mechanism in our brain. As we know from Chapter 4, this doesn't always serve our success.

The automated nature of habits means we can often overlook the significant impact that our own behaviour has in helping, or hindering, our success. The more we understand about how to form habits that help secure our future success, the less effort we need to expend, and the more effective we become.

Over the past two decades, science has taken an increasing interest in exploring how habits work, and how they can be controlled to work as our ally and not the enemy.

This matters since making the right choices that move us forward, in the moments that matter, is what makes results happen.

Building successful habits that get the job done means moving beyond the usual fist pumping rah-rah and motivational hot air that we usually hear about habits for example: they take 21 days to build, if you believe you can achieve, or worse still, just visualise success and the universe will make it happen. These approaches exude inspiration but lack the motivational science to make any real difference.

It is important to understand the mental frameworks that form habits and automate the specific behaviours that advance people and performance. Just as you don't have to be a mechanic to know how to drive a car, you don't have to hold a PhD in psychology to grasp the fundamentals of habit formation. Just knowing some key principles, and one very important process, can make all the difference between making an effort and making an impact.

Habits get formed because the brain is looking for ways to reduce the effort we have to make to get things done. This energy saving instinct enables the brain to complete certain tasks automatically and then switch on for more important tasks that require higher levels of attention. Tasks such as: securing a sale, crunching the numbers, comforting a friend in crisis or delivering an important presentation.

However, sometimes the habits we build to conserve our mental energy can be counterproductive. Being afraid is a habit. So is being lonely. Waiting for more information is a habit. So is sitting on the couch as soon as you get home. Good habits reduce our workload and help us get the job done. Bad habits are often the shortcuts we have learned to take to avoid doing the more difficult work.

Being conscious of our established patterns of behaviour is critically important because once a habit is formed, the brain is no longer fully participating in the decision making process. The habits we have formed happen automatically. So without understanding the habits that drive our decisions, making any positive change that advances our success will prove to be very difficult.

Definable Moments

When we pay attention and consciously create new habits that serve the results we seek, we force the more unhelpful behaviours into the background. By building new neurological pathways we can develop more effective routines and behaviours, that research shows, becomes automated like any other habit.

Creating supportive habits that help manage the moments we find difficult, or derail our effort, is incredibly important. The more habits we instill that help manage the definable moments, the more we automate the very behaviours that help us advance. Our neural pathways learn to leverage our natural ability, enabling harder work to be done with less effort. When the work is easier to do, we engage in it more often, and significantly impact our performance integrity.

So the question we need to be asking is: How do habits form and how can I change them? The answer relates directly to the overwhelming research over the past ten years regarding neural plasticity and the brain's ability to change.

Our brains are filled with billions of neurons that connect to each other to form neural pathways. As we do things, electrical currents run along these neural pathways making connections. The more we perform a particular action, the stronger the neural connection, and the more deeply ingrained the behaviour becomes. Just like a consistent flow of water can create a distinctive pattern in the landscape over time, neurons that fire together wire together.

Think about this in the context of learning to drive. In the beginning, driving is new and the neural pathways are not particularly strong, so the message travels slowly. When first learning to drive we had to really concentrate on what we were doing. The more driving we did, the more we reinforced the neural network and the easier driving became. This continued to the extent where we now can have a conversation with someone, conjure up a plan for dinner and change the radio station as we drive home from work. The act of driving has become an automated behaviour based on a series of strong neural connections that have been cemented in your brain. These connections occur over time through a process we commonly know as the habit loop.

THE HABIT LOOP

Charles Duhigg is a New York Times journalist who has written a practical and compelling book called *The Power of Habit*. Full of case studies that are backed up by neuroscience, the core premise of the book is based around what Duhigg refers to as the habit loop. A three part process within our brain that controls how habits are formed. Here is how he explains habit formation in the book:

"The process in our brain is a three step loop. Firstly, there is a trigger or cue that tells your brain to go into automatic mode and which habit to use. Then there is the routine, which can be physical, mental or emotional. Finally, there is a reward that helps your brain figure out if this habit loop is worth remembering for the future."

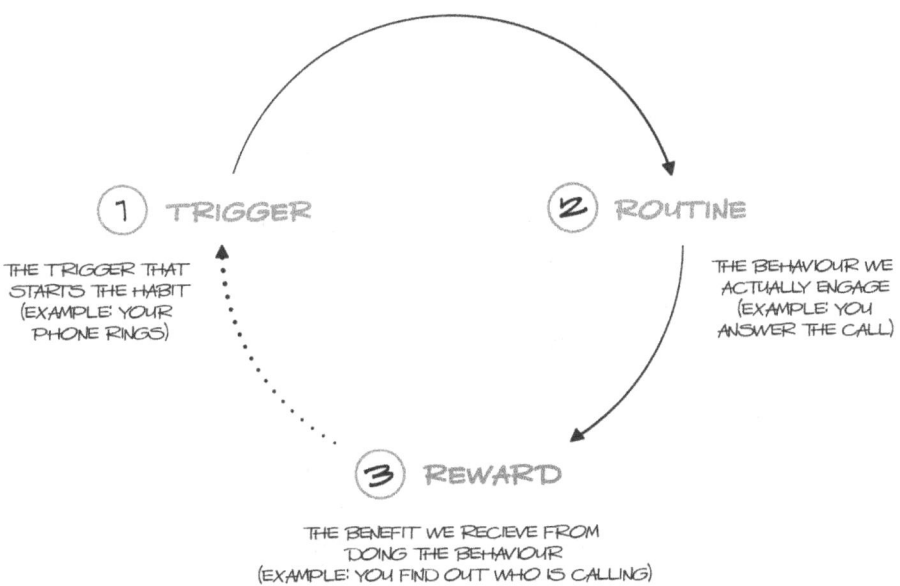

Figure 14: Habits are formed by a three-step loop.

Every habit you have follows this same three-step process, which starts to look even more compelling when you overlay the equally important decision making process of *Event x Choice = Outcome* explained in Chapter 4. The **trigger (event)** that starts the habit, the **routine (choice)** is the behaviour we engage, and the **reward (outcome)** is the benefit we receive from doing the behaviour. Here are three examples of how the right habit loop can help foster high performance:

Definable Moments

A Reputation Habit:

TRIGGER: A problem is raised
ROUTINE: You offer your insights
REWARD: You enhance your reputation

A Productivity Habit:

TRIGGER: A request is made
ROUTINE: You avoid the automatic yes
REWARD: You take control of your time

A Performance Habit:

TRIGGER: Something gets hard
ROUTINE: You put your skills to work
REWARD: You build the capability for results

Contrary to popular belief, success is not attained through a series of disciplined decisions we choose to make every day. Success is achieved by building a series of successful habit loops that move us forward in the definable moments. When we build the habits that automate performance behaviours in the moments that matter, we make results happen. We program our neural pathways to leverage the preloaded responses that work to advance performance.

One of the biggest barriers we have in achieving any level of success is backing ourselves and believing we are good enough. We tend to accentuate the belief that successful people have more talent, discipline or direction. But this just isn't the case. They have merely honed their habits to behave a certain way.

Michael Phelps was not always a disciplined and focused athlete. Suffering ADHD from an early age he was often restless, disruptive and in trouble. Bob Bowman, his coach since age eleven, said: "Michael spent most of his time on the side of the pool near the lifeguard stand for disruptive behaviour." Hardly the attributes many coaches would look for in a potential Olympic champion.

However, at the time of his retirement, Phelps was the most decorated athlete in Olympic history. He had set dozens of world records, won 22 gold medals and broke the previous record held by Mark Spitz of winning eight gold medals at Beijing in 2008. Bob Bowman had built a series of habits over the course of Phelps' career that set him apart and made Phelps the strongest mental competitor in the pool.

Bob Bowman said: "If you were to ask Michael what's going on in his head before competition, he would say he's not really thinking about anything. He's just following the program. But that's not right. It's more like his habits have taken over. When the race arrives, he's more than halfway through his plan and he's been victorious at every step. All the stretches went like planned. The warm up laps were just like he visualized. His headphones are playing exactly what he expected. The actual race is just another step in the pattern that started earlier that day and has been nothing but victories. Winning is a natural extension."

The benefit to building successful habits is why some of the world's most respected companies are using the power of habits to improve performance.

Deloitte Consulting, the largest tax and financial services company in the world, train their staff in a curriculum called *Moments That Matter*. A program that teaches specific routines to staff so they can effectively manage the difficult moments associated with their work, like when a client questions their fee.

IKEA is another global store offering training to employees about managing the definable moments with specific habits to manage situations effectively. For example, when a customer comes into the store feeling overwhelmed, a staff member will ask them to visualise their space at home and describe how they will feel when everything is finished and looking fantastic.

When Deloitte employees explain their fees, or the IKEA staff member calms a customer, they know ahead of time how to respond to an identified trigger. Their habit training has taught them how to respond to the trigger of a price sensitive client or overwhelmed customer. The trigger appeared. The habit was engaged. Companies embracing this approach understand that people rarely rise to the occasion. We usually sink to our level of skill.

With nearly 40% of habits occurring automatically, many of the habits you form are subconscious. If you continually avoid difficult conversations to escape conflict, you form a habit. If you are constantly busy because it makes you feel successful, you form a habit. If you have the courage to pursue what matters to you, you also form a habit.

Finding the habits that drive behaviour can have an enormous impact on how you live your life. Not knowing how to form habits isn't the hard part here, rather the hard work is in being clear about how to form the habits that get the job done.

KEYSTONE HABITS

Not all habits are created equal. Keystone habits are the core behaviours that, once formed, reverberate out across other areas of our life, making other positive habits easier to acquire. Research has shown the more we focus on keystone habits, the more we expand our experience of achievement. Refining the keystone habits even further to concentrate on the difficult moment that often derails results, provides even greater gains to advancing performance.

To understand the powerful influence of keystone habits, consider a study conducted in 1992 by a British psychologist working inside two of Scotland's busiest orthopedic hospitals. The average patient recruited for the study was sixty-eight years old, earned less than $10,000 a year, and finished their formal education at high school. They had undergone recent hip or knee replacement surgery that was excruciating. The intrusive, and sometimes brutal nature of the operation caused patients to have considerable post-operative pain. However, getting patients to start moving, by doing the smallest of movements, after the surgery was a key indicator to the quality of their recovery.

Patients who started to move shortly after surgery, before the muscles and skin had completely healed, minimised the scar tissue around the joint that could impede future mobility. But the pain was so extreme, it was not uncommon for people to prefer inaction and avoid rehabilitation, particularly elderly patients who often refused to follow their doctor's advice.

The people recruited for the Scottish study were seen as the type of person who would fail at rehabilitation. After all, this study was designed to see if building a habit would influence rehabilitation. After surgery, the scientist conducting the experiment gave patients a booklet detailing their rehabilitation schedule. The booklet also contained thirteen additional pages, one for each week, with blank pages to record their goals for the week. Patients were asked to complete the blank pages detailing, as specifically as possible, their plans for the week.

When the researcher returned three months later to check patient's progress she found a noticeable difference between the two groups. The patients who had written plans in their booklets recovered much faster than those who didn't. They started walking again more quickly than their counterparts. Their mobility, such as using a chair unassisted, was also more advanced. They were tying their shoes, doing laundry and beginning to make their own meals much faster than those who didn't record their plans for the week ahead of time.

As the psychologist reviewed the completed booklets, she noticed two common denominators to the journal entries. Firstly, patients were using the blank pages to manage the most mundane aspects of their recovery. Like getting out of bed, walking to the toilet or walking around the ward. Secondly, patients were also writing down how they would handle a specific moment of anticipated pain. For example, the man who exercised on the way to the toilet knew the pain would be most acute when he stood up from the couch. So he committed to take his first step straight away to avoid the temptation to sit back down.

By writing up plans ahead of time, patients were building habits to manage the moments when they knew their pain, and the temptation to quit, would be strongest. Intuitively, patients were making a plan to define the definable moment.

Establishing a keystone habit to help in their recovery highlighted the specific moment patients needed to put their skills to work. As a consequence, they became better at regulating their pain impulses and the temptation to quit. Once the neural pathways for performance have been developed, the brain becomes more practiced at delivering the actions that accelerate results.

Each patient also did something else. They defined the reward they would receive from doing the difficult task that gave them pain. One patient who walked to the bus stop every day got to see his wife. The man who walked to the bathroom rewarded himself with chocolate after completing the task.

Rewards are essential for building successful habits because they form the core of our neurological function. Our brains are wired to connect our actions with the associated reward we receive. This helps us to replicate positive behaviours and turn them into habits. Without making this connection, we fail to create a complete habit loop and miss out on automating behaviours that build success.

For the patients in the Scottish study, creating a keystone habit turned the hard work of rehabilitation into something more manageable. The patients who didn't write their recovery plans could have achieved the same results. All of the patients had been made aware of how important exercise was for recovery post surgery. Each patient had spent similar time in rehabilitation.

But patients who didn't write out plans were at a disadvantage because they quit in the definable moments when their pain was most pronounced. They never designed a keystone habit to manage the most difficult moment of their recovery, including a relevant reward for doing the most painful work. Even if they intended to do the work, their commitment abandoned them as soon as they felt the pain from the first few steps.

Building keystone habits helps to accelerate our success. Failing to do so makes the hard work of success even harder, because the shortcut we inevitably take to avoid the hard work restricts our ability to achieve results.

MAKE HABITS STICK

Most of the time when we think about habits, we think about the bad ones. Constantly interrupting people, biting our nails, spending too much time on social media, or procrastinating when we need to be productive. But we also have a series of successful habits that are equally helpful to enrich our life.

Habits are critical for performance because unless you are aware of your current habits, or deliberately working to create new habits, they happen automatically. This is why so many change efforts fail. Once we develop a habit for lazing on the couch, conforming to popular opinion or avoiding personal responsibility, the behaviour occurs automatically. So do our successful habits.

The golden rule of habit change is to avoid trying to remove the bad habits we don't like. We can't prevent old habits. We can only replace old bad habits with new good habits. Habits that better serve who we are, how we behave and the work we want to do. To develop better habits, and serve the future more consciously, we need to understand the five things that make habits stick.

1. **FOCUS YOUR EFFORT**

    The cheetah that eats regularly invests time in the tall grass stalking the herd. They know targeting one dinner option is much more productive than hunting an entire herd. Habits work in precisely the same way. Trying to change too many at once results in high effort for low outcome. Avoid the temptation to overcommit by focusing on changing one habit at a time. Making the habit a keystone habit will give you the greatest returns on your effort.

2. **FIGURE YOUR TRIGGER**

    Being acutely aware of what triggers your behaviour is critical to staying in control. Habits are automated behaviours. When we fail to figure the trigger the catalyst that commences the habit, we automatically revert to our existing habit loop, missing the moment for change. This is why after a hard day, some dieters can find themselves half way through a tub of Hagen-Dazs, wondering yet again, how did this happen?

3. **START SMALL**

   Creating a new habit that is arduous, or overly complicated, gives our brain the chance to 'hack the habit'. Subconsciously finding ways to fault the new routine and return to the old preferred pattern of behaviour. Therefore, start any new habit by committing to an action that takes less than sixty seconds to do. The aim is to make the new habit so easy to do, you can't say no.

4. **ROUTINES NOT RESULTS**

   When we seek out improvement it is easy to focus on the result we want to achieve. The money we want to save. The sales we want to achieve. The job we want to secure. The result represents the outcome we want to achieve. The routines are the behaviours we practice and repeat every day, that makes the result happen. So while knowing what we want to achieve matters, success is achieved a lot easier when we build routines rather than chase results.

5. **PLAN FOR FAILURE**

   Perfectionism is a sophisticated form of procrastination. The question isn't a matter of will you fail, but when will you fail. Seeing the set back as a platform for a comeback is how successful people separate themselves. Consistency is the key. Planning for the inevitable false start or failure is smart. Making the commitment to never miss your habit twice in a row will focus your resolve.

Success requires the ability to define the difficult moments when it is easier to stop, than to step up. This kind of commitment is achieved by building a series of successful habits. Most of us get this wrong. We attempt to move forward by relying on willpower to manage the moments that matter. We tell ourselves we will skip dessert, stand up for ourselves, say no or start to work out three times a week. But this is a losing strategy.

Even when we make a start and succeed for a short period of time, eventually our willpower gets depleted, and the habits we were trying to escape, return. Except now we associate our efforts for improvement with feelings of failure and defeat. Motivation sinks, momentum stalls and success seems elusive.

Build successful habits

Successful people do things differently.

Think about it. The person who wakes up in the morning, meditates for ten minutes, has a decent breakfast, does a good days work, practices a musical instrument, then finds time to learn a new language, call their mother every Sunday, budget their finances and find time for their family, are not making conscious decisions every minute of the day against a wave of interference.

They understand the benefit of building habits. Their willpower gets invested in building successful habits that are sustainable, and serve their success. They don't try and do it all, have it all or attempt large scale seismic shifts they have no hope in maintaining day after day, month after month and year after year. They understand this approach is unlikely to work. They have achieved their success by focusing on transforming their habits.

The barrier to securing our success is not a question of talent, the time we have available or the task that needs to be done. The barrier exists in our ability to develop the high performance habits that support the results we seek. Acquiring the assets that enable us to achieve performance integrity.

6
Make Motivation Happen

If we are going to do this difficult work that drives results, we need to make motivation matter. Many of our assumptions about motivation have been manufactured in historical folklore rather than motivational science. The sophisticated nature of motivation has been lost in quick fixes, incentivised solutions and fist pumping rah-rah that reduces discretionary effort.

Motivation using well-designed work is less about inspiration and more about ambition. Without careful consideration, we can end up choosing the wrong strategy to motivate performance. Positive intentions to recognise and reward performance can backfire, creating a series of unintended consequences that contradict the very outcome we are trying to achieve. Now more than ever, results are reliant on leaders being able to make motivation matter.

Drive: The Surprising Truth About What Motivates Us by Daniel Pink highlights how much motivation has changed. Drawn from over four decades of scientific research, the book details the misconceptions about motivation, and exposes a real disconnect between what science knows and what business does.

The premise of the book highlights how carrot and stick rewards are quickly becoming redundant to motivate people to do *meaningful work*. The research detailed in the book calls into question the notion that rewarding something produces more of the behaviour you want, and punishing something gives you less of it. The science clearly demonstrates, when it comes to motivation in the modern workplace, carrots and sticks should be on the banned substance list.

There are a host of fascinating studies that prove we are not as motivated by money as we think, and contest the common thinking

Definable Moments

that providing higher rewards leads to higher performance. One study, conducted by Dan Ariely, the James B Duke Professor of Psychology and Behavioural Economics at Duke University, explored the effects of extrinsic incentives on performance.

He enrolled eighty-seven participants and gave them a range of challenges, from memorising a series of digits or solving word puzzles, to physical tasks like throwing a ball through a hoop. To incentivise performance, participants were offered three types of rewards for reaching certain levels of performance.

One third of the participants could earn a small reward for reaching their targets. One third could earn a medium sized reward and one third had the potential to earn a large cash prize. Not that dissimilar to the motivational structure that exist in most modern day workplaces. We reward the top performers, pay attention to potential, and largely ignore the low performers.

They recruited some volunteers to complete some tests and offered them varying levels of rewards for their results. Here's what happened. The people who were offered the medium monetary reward didn't perform any better than those who were offered a small one. And the participant's incentivised with the possibility of a large cash prize? Their results were worst of all. In eight of the nine activities, assessed across three experiments, higher incentives led to worse performance, leading the research team to make this observation:

Many existing institutions provide very large incentives for exactly the type of tasks we used here. Our results challenge that assumption. Our experiment suggests... that one cannot assume that introducing or raising incentives always improves performance. Indeed, in many instances, contingent incentives – the cornerstone of how business attempts to motivate – may be a losing proposition.

While offering quite a contentious perspective to reward based work, this finding is not uncommon. Similar experiments in leading universities, banks, economic schools and governments have arrived at very similar conclusions.

For tasks that require simple repetitive behaviour, where people merely follow the rules to achieve a result, offering contingent rewards can be effective. The carrot and stick approach of 'if you do this then you get that' will work. But when it comes to tasks that require even the most rudimentary cognitive skill, like collaboration or creative thinking, these kinds of motivators don't work. A point that becomes even more compelling when you consider the increasing importance of this kind of *heuristic* work that was highlighted in Chapter 2.

In fact, behavioural scientists have found that once the right remuneration has been established, monetary rewards can create a kind of behavioural alchemy. Offering a monetary reward can change the meaning we attach to work, and contaminate the intrinsic motivation we associate with the activity, inducing unintended consequences or unethical behaviour:

- In Gothenburg Sweden, when people who were interested in donating blood were provided monetary incentives, the motivation of their altruistic act was compromised, and so donation rates actually reduced.

- A highly competitive banking environment, motivated by huge financial incentives, promoted high levels of risk taking in the sub-prime mortgage market, creating a global financial crisis in 2007 and 2008.

- Ben Johnson, a single-minded sprinter was desperate to achieve the highest accolade in his sport by winning the 100m sprint at the 1988 Olympics. He cheated, was disqualified for doping and had his gold medal rescinded.

Money as a means for motivating performance can be complicated. Money is a powerful motivator up to a certain point. If you don't pay people adequately, they won't be motivated. However, using money as an incentive to increase performance for more complex tasks decreases performance. The best use of money for motivating people is to pay people enough to avoid it being an issue. So people stop thinking about the money and can start focusing on the work.

Atlassian is an Australian software company who has listened to the science and is embracing a different approach to motivation and performance. Moving away from the traditional approach of monetary incentives, founders Scott Farquhar and Mike Cannon-Brookes encourage their employees to be self-directed and take responsibility for improving performance across the business.

Once a quarter on a Thursday afternoon, engineers have the opportunity to work on anything they want, the way they want with whomever they want. Many work through the night in order to meet the 4pm deadline the following day, where people must reveal their output with the rest of the company. Not at a dull or dry workplace meeting, but an enjoyable event involving ample quantities of cold beer and cake. Atlassian refers to these self-directed days as 'FedEx days' because people have to deliver something overnight.

Giving people one day of unbridled autonomy has led to existing software issues being fixed and ideas for new products, that would usually never see the light of day, be developed. And providing people with the opportunity to focus on more purpose driven work is significant for maintaining high levels of motivation.

The rise of purpose-based motivation makes work more enjoyable and helps to retain top talent. High levels of discretionary effort get invested without the need for large incentives. Alternatively, money based motivation reinforces the belief that effort is about economics, you get what you pay for, which leads to low motivation, employee disengagement and uninspired workplaces.

Modern day motivation demands we move away from profit-based rewards and start to encourage purpose-based recognition. This flies in the face of traditional management structures where people are encouraged to be compliant. The key to creating competitive advantage comes from harnessing the motivation people feel by making progress in meaningful work.

THE POWER OF PROGRESS

For nearly fifteen years, Professor Teresa Amabile and Professor Steven Kramer have been studying how people perform complex work inside organisations. As part of their research, in 2010 they asked over 650 managers, from dozens of companies in different industries and at varying managerial levels, to rank the managerial tools that can affect employee's emotions and motivation at work.

Participants in the study ranked five tools: recognition, making progress, incentives, interpersonal support and clear goals, in order of importance.

While each of the possible options helps to promote performance, *recognition of good work* was the one factor considered by managers as most important for positively influencing motivation, which makes sense. Every employee likes to receive some recognition, either privately or publically for a job well done.

However, what Amabile and Kramer found interesting was this response directly contradicted earlier research they had conducted with employees. In the earlier study, 238 different employees from several companies were monitored over a four-month period, keeping a detailed journal about their workday. The purpose was to understand the emotional states of each employee and the workday events that correlated to the highest levels of motivation at work.

The research yielded over 12,000 journal entries. Naturally, each individual in the experiment experienced highs and lows. However, when analysing the data, Amabile and Kramer found the most important factor for employees was exactly what the managers ranked as the least effective tool: *a clear sense of progress*.

The dramatic difference between the two pieces of research highlights one of the common misconceptions regarding motivation. Managers tend to over-emphasise the importance of external motivators, like goals and rewards, and underestimate how proactively recognising progress can elevate motivation.

This difference creates one of the most common disconnects I confront when working with disengaged teams or large-scale cultural change.

Definable Moments

Leaders driving their team way too hard to achieve a specific timeline or target, failing to provide the recognition the team requires, to sustain the effort to succeed.

Chapter 3 highlighted our inability to deliver endless amounts of hard work. We don't have an endless supply of energy at our disposal. So when recognition of the results orientated work we are doing is missing, we quickly lose motivation and stop doing the very work that drives the results we desire.

When recognition is low, our motivation suffers. Without a sense of progress, work starts to feel hard, people start to feel stuck and performance stops.

We have all been there at one stage or another in our career. Being asked to invest our discretionary effort, beyond the call of duty for a client, deadline or leader in desperate need of assistance. Only to find, after the fact, the crisis was averted, the timeframe got changed or the leader discovered a new perspective, which made the time and work invested, a pointless exercise.

This is reflective of the real challenge when motivating people and performance. We only have a limited supply of energy and effort to invest in things. As we get more aware, we become subconsciously smart about where we decide to invest our discretionary effort. If the work we do isn't recognised, appears pointless or seems to have little impact, our discretionary effort starts to diminish.

The important, and often difficult work, gets replaced with the work we prefer to do and is easier to do, but is rarely the work that builds our better future.

When writing this book I experienced procaffeination. Heading to my local café to grab a coffee rather than stick with the hard work required to write a book. Other common forms of procrastination involve cleaning, exercising, baking, meeting or surfing social media. All designed to escape the more difficult work we should be doing.

We default to less demanding work when our sense of progress is low.

The work associated with our top value activities gets replaced with a low value alternative. We spend our days working hard to get things done but not necessarily working hard to get the right things done.

Replacing the tension we experience from hard work with an easier alternative, gives us a sense of progress. But defaulting to activities that reduce the tension to make us feel better doesn't necessarily mean they are better. We may have managed fifty-two emails, booked our holiday and helped out a colleague, but the valuable work that drives meaningful progress, is still waiting to be done.

This is why recognising progress is so important to performance.

The power of recognising progress compliments what the scientific research shows about workplace motivation. When we see the effort we are investing is having an impact, making a difference or moving things forward, we continue to invest effort in that work. Making progress visible enhances motivation.

In their book *Switch: how to change things when things are hard* Chip and Dan Heath cite a terrific example of an experiment conducted by a car wash chain to determine the loyalty card that gives the greatest return on investment.

Customers were divided into two groups. Every time the first group bought a car wash, they got a stamp on their card, and when they filled up their card with eight stamps, they received a free car wash. The second group of customers received a slightly different card. They needed ten stamps to gain a free car wash, but on receiving their card, employees gave them a head start by offering two free stamps straight away saying: "this will get you started".

The mathematics of both loyalty cards was the same. Buy eight washes and get one free. But the psychology was very different. The first card had customers starting from scratch, whereas the second card put customers 20% closer to achieving their goal. A few months later the results were telling: 19% of the first group had earned a free wash compared to 34% of the second, head start group. And the second group earned their free wash faster.

DEFINABLE MOMENTS

Making progress visible leverages the power of the *goal gradient effect*. Where people become more motivated the closer they are to achieving their goal. The most potent strategy that leaders can deploy to advance people and performance, is to provide a sense of progress in the definable moments when the work is being done.

It is the most under utilised strategy for turning potential into performance.

MOTIVATE WHAT MATTERS

Most of us have a strong desire to do the difficult work that gets the job done. And this matters because it runs counterintuitive to the common reward based approaches used to motivate people and performance. Modern motivational theory shows the greatest gains to performance occur when emotional labour gets reinforced. Actually recognising the difficult work that gets the job done.

Recognising progress has been replicated over and over again in a host of different experiments and the science is outstandingly clear. If the work matters to us, and is reinforced regularly, we don't need overly complicated strategies to maintain motivation. We only need to reinforce three elements that provide a sense of satisfaction from doing difficult work: recognition, rituals and rewards.

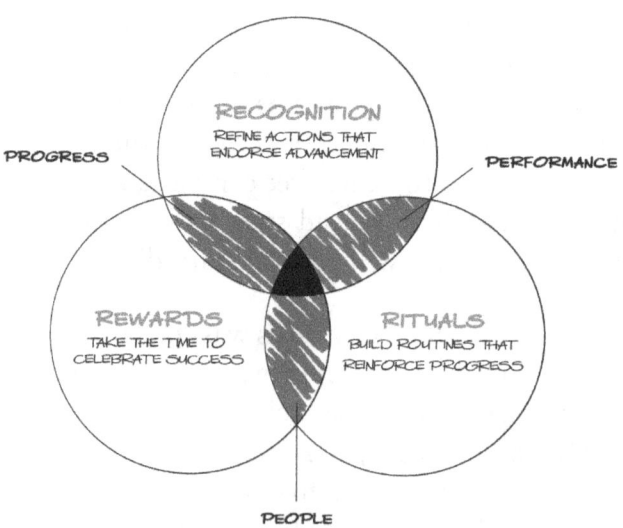

Figure 15: Three essential elements that provide a sense of progress.

Consider each of the three elements of recognition, ritual and reward to be the legs on a three-legged stool. All three need to be present to provide balance. When one element is missing the balance becomes impacted. Any imbalance creates unintended consequences. To avoid the side effects that can hinder people, progress or performance, each of the three elements needs to be present.

RECOGNITION

Recognition is the art of catching people engaging in the specific behaviours that encourage advancement. This can range from sending someone flowers to say thanks for a job well done, to arranging for the CEO to come to your next team meeting to say thanks for the work they are doing. The point is to make sure the positive contribution people are making is being regularly recognised.

Recognising positive decisions that serve the results we seek is one of the most under utilised strategies in the pursuit of success. All too often we overlook the obvious benefits to recognition, believing work is a serious business, or positive reinforcement should only be used as a reward for high performance, not as a tool for driving it. But Richmond Police Department in Canada decided to challenge this traditional thinking and started to issue Positive Tickets.

Instead of police catching young people perpetrating a crime, they would focus on catching them doing something good. Throwing rubbish in the bin not on the street, turning up to school on time, wearing a helmet if they were riding their bike, or skate boarding in the appropriate designated areas. These positive based actions were rewarded with a ticket for positive behaviour.

Each positive ticket was issued on the spot to assist young people make an immediate connection between their behaviour and the reward they received. Tickets could then be redeemed for some kind of small reward such as free entry into the movies or VIP seats to an event at the local youth center.

The initiative for the Richmond Police Department to reimagine their workplace by recognising positive behaviour, made a real impact.

It took some time, but with a conscious effort to implement the Positive Ticket system, the crime rate reduced and incidents of people reoffending decreased from 60% to 8%. Catching people doing things right created a much safer community.

RITUALS

Rituals are the formal routines we integrate into our work to recognise progress. This might take the form of an online roadmap, Gantt chart on the wall, post match review, or monthly stand up meeting. Form is less important than function. Regular rituals provide the important opportunity to connect people with a sense of progress. They are the consistent routines that help to calibrate our energy and effort, in order to maximise our impact.

A client of mine had recently been appointed the Chief Operating Officer of a large multinational corporation. He had responsibility for twenty-six different business units, operating across three time zones, with thirteen direct reports. He was constantly busy so came to me craving some solutions to manage the workload that had become all too consuming.

As a senior leader within the business, he had been to every time management training session, and was skeptical about the usual tools and techniques he had heard before and tried to implement. So we decided to take another approach. With some planning, and his blessing, I gathered his direct reports into a room, laid out his monthly calendar on the large Boardroom table, and asked the team to find my client ten more hours a week. They were positively brutal.

The team spent three hours challenging his priorities, questioning his need for control and cutting back the unnecessary meetings, conference calls and catch ups they believed were unnecessary for his role. At the end of the meeting we had found thirteen hours of legitimate time that could be saved by embracing some of the insights suggested by the team. This process proved so positive, it has become a monthly ritual he undertakes to stay on top of his time.

And this is the point of the ritual – to find some strategies that help reinforce a sense of progress in the work that matters to you. Done well, these strategies don't need to be overly technical or tedious. They just need to ensure progress has visibility and accountability.

REWARDS

Done well, offering recognition and rituals will provide adequate doses of inherent motivation, so this final element focuses more on extrinsic rewards: the benefits, bonuses or brilliant ideas we can execute to celebrate achieving a positive outcome. Initiatives that have the greatest impact tend to make a direct connection between the hard work and high achievement.

The world of work is shifting away from payment-based motivation to use more purpose-based motivation. Where recognition and rituals reinforce work being done making the work itself inherently motivating. That said, when deciding to use rewards, consider these three things so they have the desired impact:

Budget. Bigger isn't always better. I've seen someone start to cry from a thoughtful hand written letter they received recognising the work they have done. Equally, a client of mine takes their top twenty performers every year overseas for a unique travel experience. Both can be effective.

Flexibility. Money works as a motivator but being creative when rewarding people sends an even more compelling message. Giving someone a paid day off, tickets to a VIP event, car park space for the week or sending flowers to their family because they have worked late, also communicates you care. It also avoids the 'alchemy issue' where money can cheapen meaningful work.

Variability. Avoid being predictable. I worked for a leader we called Willy Wonka due to his habit of dishing out chocolate as a reward. Giving the same types of reward, at a similar time, for the same types of things makes rewards predictable, and so they lose impact. The golden rule for rewards is variability. Mixing things up will serve you much better than being predictable.

There is one final thing to remember with giving rewards. Always consider what the recipient would enjoy rather than what you would enjoy. Racing around a go-cart track might appeal to your sense of adventure, but will probably horrify the office introvert. Rewards work best when they resonate with the recipient.

The three elements of recognition, ritual and reward are just like the legs on a three-legged stool. All three need to be present to provide balance. When one element is missing, the balance is impacted and some unintended side effects can occur that hinder people, progress or performance.

- When we fail to recognise actions **people** take that support advancement, personal contributions appear pointless, and so people stop doing the work.

- When we fail to build routines that reinforce **progress** people are making, the exertion of effort creates fatigue, so people stop doing the work.

- When we fail to take time to celebrate the **success** that has been achieved, accolades of achievement are overlooked, so people stop doing the work.

If the difficult work that drives results is not being done, problems can often be overcome by assessing behaviour through the lens of recognition, rituals and rewards. These are the three elements that make work **work**, and provide a powerful diagnostic for assessing performance. When one of the elements is missing, motivation is reduced and results begin to deteriorate.

Successfully integrating recognition, rituals and rewards into the difficult work that drives results, brings modern day motivational theory to life. When we stop using the usual motivational hype that sounds good, but rarely does much good, we can start to embrace the science of success that is proven to significantly increase the probability of performance.

MAKE WORK MEANINGFUL

Prior to my last year of high school I started a part-time job at a plastics factory. For eight hours a day, I sat stationary at a bench breaking small plastic needles from a mold and separating the good ones from faulty ones. Each small needle was destined for the Porsche factory in Germany to be fitted as a speedometer in some of the world's most expensive cars.

Regardless of how hard I worked, or how efficient I became, there were always more needles to break, sort and stack. The days were long, the work seemed pointless and so my level of satisfaction was almost non-existent. Receiving a salary at the end of every month was the only thing that sustained my effort.

Despite many modern day jobs having more opportunity to provide autonomy, creativity and challenge, motivation can often be impaired because leaders fail to make the work meaningful. Worse still, sometimes we lose our own way and see work as something to be endured while waiting for the weekend to unwind and engage in the activities that ignite our passion and give us a sense of progress.

This is the final piece to the motivational puzzle. Making progress in pointless work where we feel devalued, demotivated and frustrated does nothing to maintain motivation. We must be making progress in *meaningful work*. The work we do that has an impact, makes a difference or moves things forward.

In 1983, Steve Jobs was trying to lure John Sculley away from his successful role at PepsiCo, to become CEO of Apple and apply his significant marketing skills to the personal computer market. Famously, Jobs sealed the deal by asking Sculley: "Do you want to spend the rest of your life selling sugared water or do you want a chance to change the world?" In making his successful pitch, Jobs leveraged the psychological force every human holds: the desire to do meaningful work.

Fortunately, we don't have to be changing the world for work to be meaningful. We just need to feel like we are making progress in work that matters to us. If you have ever cooked a complex meal, completed a marathon, secured a new client, attended a public rally, or convinced your child to eat their vegetables; you know what it's like to do meaningful work.

Motivation spikes when we are engaging in meaningful work. Work that seems difficult when we are trying to get it done, but proves to be worthwhile when we succeed and experience a sense of achievement. Whether you are managing people or trying to motivate yourself into action, there are nine things we need to consider to ensure work remains meaningful and motivating.

1. ATTENTION

Progressing work that matters and is meaningful requires periods of focused attention. This can prove very difficult in a world where we have an abundance of information and a shortage of attention. The constant stream of distraction and disruption can divert our attention from our most valuable work. We need to create the time, space or conditions to do our most important work.

A leader of mine used to place a large witch's hat at his office door to create a distraction free workspace. Some people power up the laptop when they fly. A client of mine works out of his local café for a few hours one morning a week. The point is to design a period of peak productivity so you can give focus to the six small tasks, or one massive milestone, that needs to get done.

2. FEEDBACK

Feedback is a fundamental tool for peak performance. Real time feedback, where we gain information in close proximity to the work we are doing, is a brilliant mechanism for maintaining focus. Rather than worrying about whether we are doing something right, we can remain immersed in the task we are doing. The faster feedback is provided the greater the impact on performance.

Traditional Japanese martial arts used to have two belt grades – a white belt for beginners and a black belt for masters. It would take approximately ten years of hard work and dedicated practice to earn a black belt until the USA Marines introduced their belt grading system.

Breaking down specific skills into belts that provided a clear sequence for skill development, and focused feedback, enabled the marines to obtain their black belts in a fraction of the time.

3. CHALLENGE

Boredom can blunt motivation. But the right level of novelty, unpredictability or complexity can maximise the attention we bring to a task. Finding the right level of stretch helps to sustain our focus and attention because we are forced to work beyond default thinking and behaviour. Psychologists refer to achieving the right balance as The Goldilocks Principal. Seeking opportunities to expand our skills and contribution is critical for securing results and staying relevant.

Motivation is greatest when we are working somewhere between stretch and strain. If the work is too menial, our attention disengages and we miss the opportunity to make a difference. If the work is too hard, fear can escalate and so we begin to search for ways to extricate ourselves from the work to be done. Motivation is maintained when the challenge is greater than the skill we bring.

4. AUTHENTICITY

When we are engaged in meaningful work, we rarely are in breach of the values or behaviours that matter in our life. We are not afraid to take a stand, share an idea or challenge an opinion, because our core values are consistently visible. We make a positive impact by investing the assets we have in work that we do.

At the peak of their powers, Steve Jobs and Bill Gates ran two very successful, but very different computer companies. The companies were profitable because the leaders were authentic and the products reflected their values. Authenticity is the greatest ally for pursuing personal and professional advancement. We can fail to progress when we are trying to emulate someone else. Watching others and learning from what they do is healthy. Staying true to you is heroic.

5. AMPLIFICATION

The basic premise of good improvisation is to build on a scenario that has been established. When someone opens with: "There are raindrops on my wedding dress," then: "I can't see them," is an unhelpful response. Denial and negativity do nothing for making a scene exciting. But when the reply is additive: "I can see that, but the toilet paper stuck to your shoe is what I would be worried about," amplifies the options and makes for an interesting story.

Meaningful work can often exist at the edges of what is do-able or possible. Just like improv theatre, progress gets a helpful push when interactions are additive rather than argumentative. Expecting to achieve immediate perfection, strategic alignment or personal success can set the bar too high. We end up feeling like we are not making progress and quit because we lose motivation. Momentum is best achieved when information, ideas and actions are amplified.

6. RECALIBRATION

Feeling over-committed once in a while because you are stretching yourself for something meaningful can often be the sign of an exciting life. Doing it all the time creates burnout. The emotional exhaustion that comes from keeping up appearances, working yourself ragged or having people overly reliant on you. High performers are acutely aware that periods of effort also need periods of rest, reflection and recalibration for continual learning and growth.

You don't have to take an expensive holiday or trek for seven days and sit on a mountaintop to find time for recalibration. The practice works most effectively when we use practical strategies that we perform regularly. Strategies built into our days that promote a period of recovery after exerting our energy and effort.

7. AUTONOMY

Our level of contribution increases when we are offered challenges that stretch our competence and ability to make decisions. When the work to be done is clear, our focus is directed towards achieving the task, not spending time trying to second guess someone else's position or preference. Our full capability and concentration can be invested in work that matters and makes an impact.

Many organisations are adopting the ROWE philosophy – Results Only Work Environment. Developed by two former HR Executives, Cali Ressler and Jody Thompson, the approach encourages leaders to create the conditions where people can do their best work. People have complete autonomy over when, where and how they do their work, rather than be restricted by an over application of policies, procedures and protocols, which douse passion and slow down progress.

8. CONSEQUENCE

When we are working on tasks that have high levels of consequence, we don't need to concentrate extra hard to maintain our motivation. The elevated levels of risk ensure we do that automatically. Our prehistoric survival instinct ensures we dedicate all of our energy and attention to the task at hand. An adventure athlete might need to abseil a cliff to experience this feeling, but for the office introvert, it could arise as soon as they hear the words team offsite.

We rally in moments of crisis. We find energy and reserves to get things done that we didn't think we had. Next time you need a burst of effort because your motivation is low, lay down the law, offer yourself an ultimatum or create some internal tension. Manufacturing a crisis can do wonders for building motivation.

9. CONNECTIONS

Acquiring knowledge and a deeper understanding as to why we do certain things is a pre-requisite for positive change. Particularly when talking about repetitive patterns of behaviour, or situations we find ourselves in that don't seem to be serving us very well. This means paying attention and making the connection to patterns of behaviour that serve continual improvement.

Shawn Anchor in his book *The Happiness Advantage* refers to this as The Tetris Effect. The ability of our brain to scan the environment and search for patterns that both help and hinder our success. Sustaining a positive trajectory towards the results we seek requires us to take an honest inventory of the skills we have, the skills we need to discontinue, and the skills we need to develop.

Doing our most meaningful work can often be challenging. Despite working hard, we can easily be pulled off course by a demanding boss, difficult client, mistakes being made, or the colleague who purposefully tries to sabotage our success. These are all issues that form friction points that impact our willingness to work.

This is why making progress visible is so important.

We all have a strong intrinsic motivation to do meaningful work. However, when the going gets tough, we need reassurance that the work we are doing is making a difference, or our attention and activity will default to less difficult work. Using recognition, rituals and rewards effectively is the mechanism that maintains our motivation to do the work that delivers results.

7
Do the work

Jason is a personal trainer who works from the park near where I live. He trains a small group of people who turn up every morning looking for guidance to reach their fitness goals. The group is unaware that, despite turning up each morning, their goals will remain unfulfilled if they continue to work with Jason.

Jason turns up to each training session knowing some people will succumb to fatigue and so fail to invest the effort that real results take. Frustrated by his client's lack of fortitude, Jason does the bare minimum. He sets the exercises, keeps people to time, counts push-ups and conveys a word of encouragement, but he fails to do the hard work that would make him valuable.

The highly respected and sought after personal trainer who delivers results that keep people coming back, does more than marshal activities and keep time.

She delivers results by investing her discretionary effort in the definable moments. She takes risks and challenges people to push beyond their limits. She challenges lifestyle choices, and where necessary, helps people manage the injuries and excuses that arise, as clients work to achieve their goals. She does the work that delivers results, delights her customers and drives her reputation.

This kind of work is easy to avoid. We can hide from our vulnerability, fear and worry by putting our head down, keeping busy and staying safe. We can also fail to take responsibility for the results we want by blaming someone or something else. We feel busy, and like we are working hard, but in reality, we are hiding. Hiding from the genuine hard work that real results take.

Definable Moments

Chapter 2 highlighted the principles of modern day performance, and how defining the definable moments, has become a critical skill for the future of work. The menial and mundane work is being outsourced, outdated or made redundant. Our ability to understand the purpose of our work, and have a passion to do it exceptionally well, is the ultimate competitive advantage.

This is the problem for Jason. It could also be a problem for you.

Believing your job is a list of prescribed tasks that you deliver on spec to keep the people who pay you happy is a mistake. The job is just the work you do. It might require a qualification or certain skills, but it's the job. Finding our best in the definable moments, when results get realised, delivers value. Failing to invest our skills in these moments creates a performance liability.

Our individual liability can be found in the recurring moments that make us feel frustrated. Times when interference appears and we find things hard, we feel a little stuck and we want to stop. Times when consciously or otherwise, we choose to maintain the status quo rather than pursue our highest purpose.

The key to advancement is being able to identify the definable moments and be brave enough to impact them. Committing our skills to pursue advancement is what enables us to achieve. This rarely presents as a positive opportunity to perform. Most of the time results get disguised in difficult work. Work that demands we pursue what matters, practice discernment, stretch our existing skills and overcome our deepest fears to forge ahead in the face of doubt.

Work we choose to seek out if success is a serious aspiration.

Go. Make an Impact.

Thanks for reading *Definable Moments*.

I hope this book has had the kind of impact where you took the time to scribble some notes in the margin, highlight a section, dog-ear a page or start a conversation with your friends, colleagues, social networks or book club. Books worth buying are often books worth sharing.

When you make the courageous choice to make an impact, amazing things can happen. So whether you have a seat on the Board, work in your own business, or want a new challenge within your existing role, I trust this book has provided a platform for action.

Reading is one thing. Results are another thing entirely. If you feel inspired, but need further support to advance your aspiration, then please get in touch. My passion and purpose is to support motivated leaders who want to make results happen.

Andrew

> Find out more at:
> **www.andrewhorsfield.com**
> or say hello@andrewhorsfield.com

Book philanthropy

Books worth buying are often books worth sharing. Once you've finished reading this copy, add a name to the list (remembering to cross your name off first) and forward the book onto someone else.

Alternatively, leave it somewhere public, with a note, for someone else to pick up. You'll become a book philanthropist. Curating ideas by enabling multiple people to benefit from this single copy with the author's blessing.

_____
_____
_____
_____
_____
_____
_____
_____
_____
_____
_____
_____

This book belongs to...

_____

...and they would like it back at the end!

ORDER

Definable Moments

Andrew Horsfield

ISBN: 9781925367959   Qty

RRP   AU$ 29.99 .....

Postage within Australia   AU$5.00   .....

TOTAL* $_____

* All prices include GST

Name: ....

Address: ....

....

Phone: ....

Email: ....

Payment: [ ] Money Order   [ ] Cheque   [ ] MasterCard   [ ] Visa

Cardholder's Name:..

Credit Card Number: ....

Signature:...

Expiry Date: ....

Allow 7 days for delivery.

Payment to: Marzocco Consultancy (ABN 14 067 257 390)
                PO Box 12544
                A'Beckett Street, Melbourne, 8006
                Victoria, Australia
                admin@brolgapublishing.com.au

Be Published

Publish through a successful publisher.
Brolga Publishing is represented through:
• National book trade distribution, including sales, marketing & distribution through Dennis Jones and Associates Australia.
• International book trade distribution to
  • The United Kingdom
  • North America
  • Sales representation in South East Asia
• Worldwide e-Book distribution

For details and enquiries, contact:
Brolga Publishing Pty Ltd
markzocchi@brolgapublishing.com.au
PO Box 12544
A'Beckett St VIC 8006

ABN: 46 063 962 443
(Email for a catalogue request)

www.ingramcontent.com/pod-product-compliance
Lightning Source LLC
Chambersburg PA
CBHW050635160426
43194CB00010B/1685